To Nondas Lorraine Surber

The Gold Star Family Album 1968

In memory of your
mother 1968.
Love.

The Gold Star Family Album 1968

Edited by

Arthur and Nancy DeMoss

Art Director

H. Marie King

FLEMING H. REVELL COMPANY
WESTWOOD — NEW JERSEY

ACKNOWLEDGMENTS

Grateful acknowledgment is hereby expressed to all those who have contributed to this book. Any inadvertent omissions of credit will be gladly corrected in future editions. A few of the unsigned articles were written by the editors. Most of the items without bylines, however, are anonymous.

"To Our Guest." Reprinted by permission of Dodd, Mead & Company, Inc. from *"Silver Saturday"* by Nancy Byrd Turner. Copyright 1937 by Nancy Byrd Turner; Copyright renewed.

"A Land That Man Has Newly Trod" by Joaquin Miller. Used by permission of Juanita Miller.

The following selections by Henry van Dyke are reprinted with the permission of Charles Scribner's Sons: "Keeping Christmas" from *The Spirit of Christmas;* and "Peace Hymn of the Republic" from *Grand Canyon and Other Poems* (Copyright 1914 Charles Scribner's Sons; renewal copyright 1942 Tertius van Dyke)

"Pilgrimage" . . . "Garments Hem" . . . "So Long As There Are Homes" . . . "I Think That God Is Proud" . . . "Friends Are Like Flowers" from *Poems of Inspiration and Courage,* Grace Noll Crowell, copyright © by Grace Noll Crowell, Harper & Row, Publishers, Inc., New York.

"Mothers Never Change" by George Beverly Shea. Reprinted by permission of *Psychology for Living.*

"Dirt Farmer" by Arden Antony. Reprinted by permission of *The Christian Science Monitor.*

"Thanksgiving," "God's World" by Edna St. Vincent Millay from *Collected Poems,* Harper & Row. Copyright 1913, 1939, 1940, 1967 by Edna St. Vincent Millay and Norma Millay Ellis.

"What God Hath Promised," "To A Friend In Trouble," and "The Cross and The Tomb" by Annie Johnson Flint. Copyright. Reproduced by permission. Evangelical Publishers, Toronto, Canada.

Laurie Lee Messrs. John Lehmann, Ltd. "April Rise" from *The Bloom of Candles.*

"The Promised Land" by Marie Antin. Reprinted by permission of Houghton Mifflin Company.

"Freedom from Fear" by Stephen Vincent Benet, Copyright 1943, by The Curtis Publishing Company. Reprinted by permission of Brandt & Brandt.

"Humility" by W. Waldemar W. Argow; "A Gift of Light" by D. Luben; "Truly Great Treasures"; "The Most Beautiful Thing"; "The Tread of Footsteps" by Gertie Fry; "I Remember" by Dina Donohue; "Finding Happiness"; "Prayer and Courage Overcome Insurmountable Obstacles" reprinted by permission of *Sunshine* Magazine.

My Work from the *Searching Wind* by Ruby Jones. Copyright 1964, Warner Press, Inc. Used by permission of Warner Press.

"Sheer Joy," "I Met God In The Morning" from *Spiritual Hilltops* by Ralph S. Cushman. Abingdon Press.

"God Has Been Good To Me"—1956 by R. M. Good. Reprinted with permission from *Success Unlimited,* America's leading Success Magazine, 5050 Broadway, Chicago, Illinois 60640, copyright 1956. Further reprint rights reserved.

"For These I Give Thanks" by Sherry Brion Zearfaus. Reprinted with permission from *The Sunday Bulletin* Magazine. Copyright 1967 Bulletin Company.

"We Give Thee Thanks" by Charlotte M. Kruger. Reprinted from *Moody Monthly.* Used by permission.

"Christmas Comfort" by Mary J. Vine. Reprinted by permission of *Signs of the Times.*

"God Give Me Joy" by Thomas Curtis Clark. Reprinted through permission of First Church of Christ, Scientist, Maywood, Illinois.

"The Book That Converted Its Author" by Elizabeth Rider Montgomery. Reprinted by permission of Dodd, Mead & Company, Inc. from *The Story Behind Great Books* by Elizabeth Rider Montgomery. Copyright 1946 by Elizabeth Rider Montgomery.

"How To Grow Old Gracefully" from *Friends of God* by Costen J. Harrell. Copyright renewal 1958 by Costen J. Harrell. Used by permission of Abingdon Press.

"Awake" reprinted by permission of *Full Gospel Business Men's Voice.*

"What Easter Means To Me" by Larry Ward. Reprinted by permission of *Psychology for Living.*

"We Give Thee Thanks" by Charlotte M. Kruger. Reprinted from *Moody Monthly.* Used by permission.

"A Mighty Bulwark" from *The Face of Millions* by John A. O'Brien. Reprinted by permission of Our Sunday Visitor.

"The Meaning of Easter" by Robert J. Hastings. Used by permission of the author.

"In the Bleak Mid-Winter" by Kathleen Blanchard from *Stories of Beautiful Hymns.* Copyright 1942, Zondervan Publishing House. Used by permission of Zondervan Publishing House.

"Threshold Years" by Hannah Whitall Smith. © Copyright 1966 by The Moody Bible Institute of Chicago. Used by permission.

"Excerpt from *Valley Forge*" by Maxwell Anderson. Copyright 1934 by Maxwell Anderson. Copyright renewed 1962 by Gilda Anderson, Alan Anderson, Terence Anderson, Quentin Anderson, and Hesper A. Levenstein. All rights reserved. Reprinted by permission of Anderson House.

Hymns In Human Experience by William J. Hart (Why, That's For Me) pg-160 "What A Friend We Have In Jesus" copyright 1931 by Harper & Brothers. Reprinted by permission of Harper & Row, Publishers, Incorporated.

Hymns In Human Experience by William J. Hart (pp 30-31 "Nearer My God to Thee"). Copyright 1931 by Harper & Brothers. Reprinted by permission of Harper & Row, Publishers, Incorporated.

"Chant of Loyalty" from *Paved Streets* by Elias Lieberman, Copyright 1918, 1946 by Elias Lieberman.

Authors' Foreword

A year ago, the first *Gold Star Family Album Annual* was published. The public response has been so enthusiastic that we have been persuaded to publish a brand new, 1968 edition—with more pages, and full color.

We invite you to walk down the year with us through these pages and share more of our favorite stories, poems, hymns and nuggets.

It is our earnest prayer that you will find here inspiration and comfort for your daily life. If just one Golden Prayer or Golden Verse helps to make life more meaningful for *you*, or if you take courage from just one Golden Life, we will indeed be grateful.

Arthur and Nancy De Moss
VALLEY FORGE, PENNSYLVANIA

Contents

The Gold Star Family Album 1968

The New Year

The Gate of the New Year

I said to the man who stood at the Gate of the Year,
"Give me a light that I may tread safely into the unknown."
And he replied: "Go out into the darkness, and put your hand into the Hand of God.
That shall be to you better than light, and safer than a known way."
So I went forth,
And finding the Hand of God, trod gladly into the night.
And He led me toward the hills and the breaking of day in the lone East.
So heart be still;
What need our little life, our human life to know, if God hath comprehension,
In all the busy strife, of things both high and low,
God hideth His intention.
God knows. His will is best.
The stretch of years which winds ahead, so dim to our imperfect vision,
Are clear to God. Our fears are premature; in Him all time hath full provision.

M. L. Haskins

GOLDEN NUGGETS

I am not bound to win, but I am bound to be true. I am not bound to succeed, but I am bound to live by the light that I have. I must stand with anybody that stands right, stand with him while he is right, and part with him when he goes wrong.

Abraham Lincoln

I shall pass through this world but once. If, therefore, there be any kindness I can show, or any good thing I can do, let me do it now; let me not defer it or neglect it, for I shall not pass this way again.

De Crellet

A Psalm of Life

Tell me not, in mournful numbers,
  Life is but an empty dream!—
For the soul is dead that slumbers,
  And things are not what they seem.

Life is real! Life is earnest!
  And the grave is not its goal;
Dust thou art, to dust returnest,
  Was not spoken of the soul.

Not enjoyment, and not sorrow,
  Is our destined end or way;
But to act, that each to-morrow
  Finds us farther than to-day.

Art is long, and Time is fleeting,
  And our hearts, though stout and brave
Still, like muffled drums, are beating
  Funeral marches to the grave.

Trust no Future, howe'er pleasant!
  Let the dead Past bury its dead!
Act,—act in the living Present!
  Heart within, and God o'erhead!

Lives of great men all remind us
  We can make our lives sublime,
And, departing, leave behind us
  Footprints on the sands of time;

Footprints, that perhaps another,
  Sailing o'er life's solemn main,
A forlorn and shipwrecked brother,
  Seeing, shall take heart again.

Let us, then be up and doing,
  With a heart for any fate;
Still achieving, still pursuing,
  Learn to labor and to wait.

Henry Wadsworth Longfellow

Two Golden Days

There are two days of the week upon which and about which I never worry. Two carefree days, kept sacredly free from fear and apprehension.

One of these is YESTERDAY.

Yesterday, with all its cares and frets, with all its pains and aches, all its faults, its mistakes and blunders, has passed forever beyond the reach of my recall. I can not undo an act that I wrought; I can not unsay a word that I said yesterday.

All that it holds of my life, of wrongs, regret and sorrow, is in the hands of the Mighty God that can bring honey out of the rock and sweet waters out of the bitterest desert—the God of Love that can make the wrong things right, that can turn weeping into laughter, that can give beauty for ashes, the garment of praise for the spirit of heaviness, joy of the morning for the woe of the night.

Save for the beautiful memories, sweet and tender, that linger like perfumes of roses in the heart of the day that is gone, I have nothing to do with yesterday. It was mine; it is God's.

And the other day I do not worry about is TOMORROW.

Tomorrow with all its possible adversities, its burdens, its perils, its large promise and poor performance, its failures and mistakes, is as far beyond the reach of my mastery as its dead sister, yesterday. It is a day of God's. Its sun will rise in roseate splendor, or behind a mask of weeping clouds. But it will rise.

I have no possession in that unborn day of grace. All else is in the safe keeping of that Infinite God that holds for me the treasure of yesterday. His love is higher than the stars, wider than the skies, deeper than the seas. Tomorrow—It is God's day. It will be mine.

There is left for me then, but one day of the week—TODAY. With faith and trust in the Lord any man can fight the battles of today and any woman can carry the burdens of just one day.

O friend, it is only when to the burdens and cares of today carefully measured out to us by the Infinite Wisdom and Might that gives with them the promise, "As thy day so shall thy strength be," we willfully add the burdens of those two awful eternities—yesterday and tomorrow—that we break down. It isn't the experience of today that drives men mad. It is the remorse for something that happened yesterday, the dread of what tomorrow may disclose.

These are God's days. Leave them with Him.

Therefore, I think, and I do, and I journey but one day at a time. That is the easy day. That is man's day. Nay rather, that is our day—God's and mine. And while faithfully and dutifully I run my course, and work my appointed task on that day of ours, God the Almighty and the All-loving takes care of yesterday and tomorrow.

Robert J. Burdette

Winter

Bare old trees in silhouette
  Against a steel-gray sky;
Crisp north wind whispering
  In stately pines near by;
Jeweled frosted necklaces
  Draped on fir trees low;
Chickadees and Juncos
  Playing hide and seek below;
Sheer ice ledges bordering
  Streams meandering in meadows;
Billowy drifts of snow made ethereal
  By evening's lengthening shadows—
These are beauties that I find
  In a wonderland I scan,
And I am deeply grateful
  God included winter in His plan.

Miriam B. Nolt

Golden Thoughts

Waste no tears upon the blotted record of lost years, but turn the page and smile to see the fair white pages that remain.

So here hath been dawning another blue day; think, wilt thou let it slip useless away?

Thomas Carlyle

I see not a step before me as I tread on another year; but the past is still in God's keeping. The future His mercy shall clear, and what looks dark in the distance may lighten as I grow near.

Mary G. Brainard

Courage and Prayer Overcome Insurmountable Obstacles

During her life, Glenna Mae Hills of Logan, Ohio has displayed not only the necessary unquenchable determination to make her youthful dreams come true, but a courage that has carried her through many years of mental and physical misery. Although a victim of the misfortunes and frustrations of polio she has achieved the fulfillment of her life's hopes in a very special way.

Glenna Hills who declares she is not a "victim" has triumphed over the handicap that affected her early in life. Her valiant spirit was never defeated and today she proudly declares, "For me, polio was a blessing."

When Glenna was eleven years old, she went to a piano recital by the noted Paderewski and was thrilled as she watched his famous fingers flying over the keys. At that moment she determined that some day she, too, would become a great pianist and thrill audiences with her skill. Little did she know what was soon to follow: A raging fever, followed by months of confinement, left her body shriveled and useless.

Every treatment known to medical science was employed but to little avail. Nevertheless Glenna dreamed on; and she constantly searched her soul. She knew she was of royal blood—a descendant of brave, notable ancestors. Her father was an inventor, a genius—that she knew. What right had she—Glenna Mae Sauer—to let them all down!

Glenna gained a new perspective on life and became convinced she could write. She would become an author and thrill thousands and millions in contrast to the hundreds who might have come to hear her as a concert pianist. This new goal lifted her far above her previous dreams of success in the music world.

But Glenna knew she must use her arms to become a writer and that only she could bring them back to usefulness again. With the utmost effort she found that she could grasp the handles of an exercising machine her father had built at the foot of her bed. She exercised daily with it until she was exhausted. Then one day she discovered she could lift a book! She continued to pray fervently for strength and her prayer was answered. Finally the miracle came: Glenna had overcome her handicap and she would be able to write!

All this time she had been building up in her mind and heart a storehouse of things to write that would thrill the world and very soon her work began to appear in numerous publications. One day, Glenna received a letter from a cultured young Canadian who had picked up a magazine bearing one of her classics. He had written to tell her how impressed he was with her writing, and so began a beautiful romance that was to culminate in the marriage of Glenna Mae Sauer to F. Guy Hills.

Through the years these two have traveled widely, finding deep satisfaction in life's adventure. Says Glenna happily, "Never has it been necessary to evade a task." Such was the triumph of a valiant and unconquerable spirit.

Faith Is A Mighty Fortress

We look ahead through each changing year
With mixed emotions of
Hope and *Fear,*
Hope for *The Peace* we long have sought,
Fear that *Our Hopes*
will come to naught . . .
Unwilling to trust in the *Father's Will,*
We count on our logic and shallow skill
And, in our arrogance and pride,
Man is no longer satisfied
To place his confidence and love
With *Childlike Faith*
in God above . . .
But tiny hands and tousled heads
That kneel in prayer by little beds
Are closer to the dear Lord's heart
and of *His Kingdom*
more a part
Than we who search and never find
The answers to our questioning mind,
For faith in things we cannot see
Requires a child's simplicity . . .

Helen Steiner Rice

The New Year

A flower unblown; a book unread;
A tree with fruit unharvested;
A path untrod; a house whose rooms
Lack yet the heart's divine perfumes;
A landscape whose wide border lies
In silent shade beneath the skies;
A wondrous fountain yet unsealed;
A casket with its gifts concealed—
This is the Year that for you waits
Beyond tomorrow's mystic gates.

Horatio Nelson Powers

Friendship

My Work

Today this is my work. No special skill, no talent great is needed. No mountain-shaking task is mine, so small it seems, so very insignificant, yet let me feel that it is heaven-sent.

Oh, may I be calm and kind! May my irritation be replaced with assurance that I am an instrument through which God's hand may move, His voice may speak. Perhaps my task is humble, but the way I do it may inspire some other one to do his well—a task that's greater far than mine.

Or, I may greet a man or woman, boy or girl, who yearns for just a word of hope, a smile of cheer. These may I offer as I hurry by. Just one am I, but one of millions strong.

May what I do reach out and touch the good of them until in unity we stand, arms linked around the world. In my small niche may I with pride and love serve well—through this, my work.

Ruby A. Jones

The Poet's Prayer

If there be some weaker one,
Give me strength to help him on;
If a blinder soul there be,
Let me guide him nearer Thee;
Make my mortal dreams come true
With the work I fain would do;
Clothe with life the weak intent,
Let me be the thing I meant;
Let me find in Thy employ,
Peace that dearer is than joy;
Out of self to love be led,
And to heaven acclimated,
Until all things sweet and good
Seem my natural habitude.

John Greenleaf Whittier

I Am the Boy

Ira D. Sankey had finished singing that noble song, "Rescue the Perishing."

Said Sankey, "Years ago Fanny Crosby, the blind song writer, went to the Jerry McAuley Mission in New York City, and asked if there was a motherless boy in the audience."

Back in the rear a little fellow came forward, and the great Fanny laid her tender hands on his head and then kissed him.

"Then Fanny," continued Sankey, "went home and wrote that song, 'Rescue the Perishing,' from the inspiration of the meeting."

Sankey finished telling the story in the St. Louis mission, and then a man got up and told this story:

"I am the boy she kissed that night. I never was able to get away from the impression made by that touching act, until I became a Christian. I am now living in this city with my family, am a Christian, and am doing a good business."

The results of a tender act of compassion are inestimable. A kind word, spoken in charity, will start echoes rolling that will strike the hilltops of eternity and reverberate throughout all eternity.

To Our Guest

If you come cheerily,
Here shall be jest for you;
If you come wearily,
Here shall be rest for you.

If you come borrowing,
Gladly we'll lend to you;
If you come sorrowing,
Love shall be shown to you.

Under our thatch, friend,
Place shall abide for you;
Touch but the latch, friend,
The door shall swing wide for you!

Nancy Byrd Turner

Friendship

Stories will always be told of wise old kings who ruled tiny kingdoms back in the mythical days before the pyramids of Egypt were plotted or the grandeur of Greece gave way to the glory of Rome. And one is told of a widowed king left with twin sons. To determine while he still lived which should succeed him on the throne, the king devised a "fitness" test. He explained to them that no man could hope to hold the kingdom who did not have a host of true friends.

"Go forth," he commanded them, "and during this year see how many friends each of you can gather around you."

Junius immediately pressed his father to grant him ample funds so that he need not be embarrassed in cultivating the people who counted. It was done. Senius asked nothing, but walked away, his brows furrowed in thought.

During the months that followed the palace rang with revelry as Junius entertained. Young men laughed at his wit, older men professed to marvel that one so young could be so brainy. Arguments were brought to him to be settled by his superior judgment. At the games and races women admired his handsome face and athletic carriage. Many begged for his advice before placing their wagers. If one man sought to borrow money from him, two men promptly urged upon him generous loans, to be repaid when he became king.

Junius often bantered his brother for not making friends. "When I mention your name to my companions," he would say, "they laugh loudly and ask, 'Who is Senius?' "

But none of that annoyed Senius. He avoided the revelries of the palace, but, often while his brother slept late, he was consulting his father's ministers about adjusting unfair taxes. He often appeared in court to plead the cause of some poor wretch. He discussed military tactics with the soldiers in the barracks; he studied the work of laborers on public roads and buildings to see if he could not help them do more work with less effort; he talked with farmers in the vineyards and harvest fields, and with merchants in the bazaars, learning whatever he could from them; but always he seemed to have an hour to spare to visit someone who was sick.

When the year ended, the wise king ordered both sons seized and thrown into prison. He caused a story to be circulated that they had plotted to seize the throne, and were about to be exiled to a distant land. The princes were conveyed to a secret room from which they could hear all that was said in the king's audience chamber. Within an hour merchants, judges, captains and officials clamored for audience with the king. "Senius cannot be guilty," each declared. "He is our friend, and we know he is loyal to his king and father."

Some brave soldiers asked permission to join him in exile. One minister offered himself as hostage that Senius might be freed to make his own defense. Farmers and laborers grumbled that the king was unfair to believe Senius guilty.

But while hundreds came to avow their friendship for Senius, not one came forward to speak for Junius. Spies listened to the gossip in the market places and baths. Those who had got money from him denounced him as guilty. Others who had loaned him money, denied the fact with mighty oaths, fearful of being identified with the plot. Those who were cornered and had to admit that they were seen in his company frequently, pleaded that they were members of a crowd. Positively, they could not be called friends of the traitor, Junius.

In bitter disappointment Junius saw that in his hour of need none of his boon companions would come near him or admit to call him friend. Turning to his brother, he asked woefully, "How in the world did you make so many friends?"

And Senius replied: "I did not try to *make* friends. I simply tried to *be* a friend."

GOLDEN PRAYERS

God of our life, there are days when the burdens we carry chafe our shoulders and weigh us down; when the road seems dreary and endless, the skies grey and threatening; when our lives have no music in them, and our hearts are lonely, and our souls have lost their courage. Flood the path with light, we beseech Thee; turn our eyes to where the skies are full of promise; tune our hearts to brave music; give us the sense of comradeship with heroes and saints of every age; and so quicken our spirits that we may be able to encourage the souls of all who journey with us on the road of life, to Thy honor and glory. AMEN.

Give us the strength to encounter that which is to come, that we may be brave in peril, constant in tribulation, temperate in wrath, and in all changes of fortune, and down to the gates of death, loyal and loving one to another.

Robert Louis Stevenson

Forgive me, most gracious Lord and Father, if this day I have done or said anything to increase the pain of the world. Pardon the unkind word, the impatient gesture, the hard and selfish deed, the failure to show sympathy and kindly help where I had the opportunity, but missed it; and enable me so to live that I may daily do something to lessen the tide of human sorrow, and add to the sum of human happiness. AMEN.

F. B. Meyer

golden lives

The Road of the Loving Heart

When Robert Louis Stevenson died, the following anonymous tribute was written:

"Remembering the great love of his highness, Tusitala, and his loving care when we were in prison and sore distressed, we have prepared him an enduring present, this road which we have dug for ever."

In a far-off island, thousands of miles from the mainland, and unconnected with the world by cable, stands this inscription. It was set up at the corner of a new road, cut through a tropical jungle, and bears at its head the title of this article, signed by the names of ten prominent chiefs. This is the story of the road, and why it was built:

A number of years ago a Scotchman, broken in health and expecting an early death, sought out this lonely spot, because here the climate was favorable to the disease from which he suffered. He bought an estate of several hundred acres, and threw himself earnestly into the life of the natives of the island. There was great division among the many chiefs, and prolonged warfare. Very soon the chiefs found that this alien from a strange land was their best friend. They began coming to him for counsel. Though he did not bear that name, he became a missionary to them. He was their hero, and they loved and trusted him because he tried to lead them aright. And so it came about that when the wars ceased, the chiefs of both sides called him by a name of their own, and made him one of their number, thus conferring upon him the highest honour within their power.

But many of the chiefs were still in prison, because of their political views or deeds, and in constant danger of being put to death. Their sole friend was the Scotchman, whom they called Tusitala. He visited them, comforted them, repeated passages from the Scriptures to them, and busied himself incessantly to effect their release. At length he obtained their freedom, and then, glowing with gratitude, in spite of age, and loss of strength, they started directly for the estate of their benefactor, and there, in the terrible heat, they laboured for weeks in building him a road which they knew he had long desired. They did not cease their toil until their handiwork, which they called "The Road of the Loving Heart," was finished.

Not long after this the white chief suddenly died. At the news the native chiefs flocked from all parts of the island to the house, and took charge of the body. They kissed his hand as they came in, and all night sat in silence about him. One of them, a feeble old man, threw himself on his knees beside the body of his benefactor, and cried out between his sobs:

"I am only a poor black man, and ignorant. Yet I am not afraid to come and take the last look of my dead friend's face. Behold, Tusitala is dead. We were in prison and he cared for us. The day was no longer than his kindness." So the chiefs took their friend to the top of a steep mountain which he had loved and there buried him.

The civilized world mourns the great author. The name of Robert Louis Stevenson is lastingly inwrought into English literature. But the Samoans mourn in his loss a brother, who outdid all others in loving-kindness, and so long as the far-off island in the Pacific exists, Tusitala will be greatfully remembered, not because he was so greatly gifted, but simply because he was a great man. Fame dies, and honors perish, but "loving-kindness" is immortal.

To a Friend in Trouble

Dear, I would save you from it if I could;
Because I love you I would set you free
From sorrow, hardship, pain and poverty
And give you only what to me seems good.

But this is love — to smooth the upward way,
To level every hill you else must climb,
Lose you the vision from the heights sublime,
Toil's lovely guerdon at the close of day?

The butterfly must struggle to be free;
Mistaken kindness clips the chrysalis
And gives, in place of flight and airy bliss,
A premature and crippled liberty.

What might have made it truly free, its wings
Of vivid peacock tints and silken sheen —
Alas, the pity of what might have been —
Are weak and stunted, dragging, helpless things.

One loves you more than I, who loves you much;
Would I dare thwart the purposes Divine
And change that wise and tender will for mine?
Deny your plastic soul the shaping touch

Of Hands Omnipotent? Or spoil your life
And leave your wings a burden and a weight?
Strive on, nor lack the handicap of fate
That shall but make you stronger for the strife.

Annie Johnson Flint

Sharing

There isn't much that I can do, but I can share my bread with you, and I can share my joy with you, and sometimes share a sorrow, too—as on our way we go.

There isn't much that I can do, but I can sit an hour with you, and I can share a joke with you, and sometimes share reverses, too—as on our way we go.

There isn't much that I can do, but I can share my flowers with you, and I can share my books with you and sometimes share your burdens, too—as on our way we go.

There isn't much that I can do, but I can share my songs with you, and I can share my mirth with you, and sometimes come and laugh with you—as on our way we go.

There isn't much that I can do, but I can share my hopes with you, and I can share my fears with you, and sometimes shed some tears with you—as on our way we go.

There isn't much that I can do, but I can share my friends with you, and I can share my life with you, and ofttimes share a prayer with you—as on our way we go.

Maude V. Preston

A Prayer

Teach me, Father, how to go
Softly as the grasses grow;
Hush my soul to meet the shock
Of the wild world as a rock;
But my spirit, propt with power,
Make as simple as a flower.
Let the dry heart fill its cup,
Like a poppy looking up;
Let life lightly wear her crown
Like a poppy looking down.

Teach me, Father, how to be
Kind and patient as a tree.
Joyfully the crickets croon
Under shady oak at noon;
Beetle, on his mission bent,
Tarries in that cooling tent.
Let me, also, cheer a spot,
Hidden field or garden grot—
Place where passing souls can rest
On the way and be their best.

Edwin Markham

The Unfailing Friend

The friendship of Jesus is lasting. Other friends may grow old and cold. It is not so with the friendship of our Saviour. Other friends may possibly misunderstand us. Jesus never. His love is the same in youth as in old age. The friendship will rather grow stronger in old age. When you have lost what to you seemed everything, and you find yourself friendless and alone, despised and forsaken, Jesus will be your dear and precious Friend.

GOLDEN YEARS

How to Grow Old

"Grow old along with me! The best is yet to be,
The last of life for which the first was made."

Robert Browning

Nothing is sadder than not to know the truth of Browning's words, nothing more rewarding than to live by them. There is as much of the "last of life" to enjoy as the first, maybe more.

Many strong, fine, exciting things belong to youth. I'm glad I missed none of them. But they pass out of our experience in due time and we must let them go and be ready to take others just as good, or better. There are those who store nothing in those splendid, reckless young years to fill the later ones. They think of happiness in terms of what youth alone can be, and know, and do. For them, the last of life can be barren, cold, sometimes ugly in its attempts to prolong that youth.

But those who plant seeds of love, service, friendship know the last of life as a privilege, and a continuing adventure. The fevers of the blood die down, the spirit grows serene. Friendships grow deeper with shared years, memories become hallowed, beauty can be enjoyed without the torturing need of possession, humor becomes part of wisdom, and service is a gift worth offering to those still on the battlefield of youth. The harvest of work well done, of love freely given, is ripe for reaping.

The books we never had time to read, the people we never had time to talk to, the games we never watched because we were so busy playing them, the prayers we never had time to say—all these can be ours at last.

Adela Rogers St. John

GOLDEN NOTES

What a Friend We Have in Jesus

A minister's wife tells of the time when her only sister lay on a bed of pain in a hospital in one of the suburbs of Chicago. Her father and mother, being sent for, reached the bedside at nightfall. A brief interview was permitted. The father, bending low above his girl, heard her faintly say, "Oh, Dad, I've lost my grip." Great anxiety, therefore, was on his mind as he left the room.

Fearing the answer he might receive, yet hungering for news, the father telephoned as early the next morning as he dared. "How is the girl today?" was his agonized question.

"Holding her own. In fact, she has made slight progress through the night," was the glad and astonishing answer. Father and mother, therefore, soon hastened to the hospital. There they learned that the daughter's recovery was now a possibility.

Later the parents learned the cause of the happy change. A window had been opened by a nurse, and there came through it to the accompaniment of a piano a clear baritone voice singing: "What a Friend we have in Jesus!"

"Why, that's for me," whispered the sufferer, as she heard the words:

"Are we weak and heavy laden,
Cumbered with a load of care?
Precious Saviour, still our refuge,
Take it to the Lord in prayer."

Restful assurance was expressed in the closing lines:

"In His arms He'll take and shield thee,
Thou wilt find a solace there."

Making the words her prayer, by asking Christ to take and shield her, she turned her face to the wall and the first natural sleep for weeks followed. From that hour her recovery began.

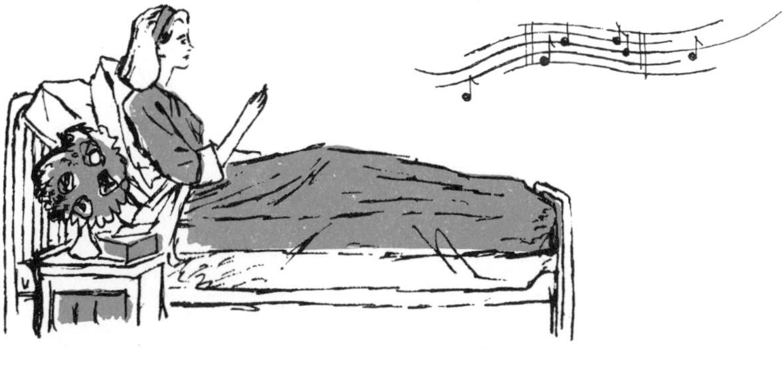

I Shall Not Pass This Way Again

I shall not pass this way again—
  Although it bordered be with flowers,
  Although I rest in fragrant bowers,
  And hear the singing
  Of song-birds winging
To highest heaven their gladsome flight;
Though moons are full and stars are bright,
And winds and waves are softly sighing,
While leafy trees make low replying;
Though voices clear in joyous strain
Repeat a jubilant refrain;
Though rising suns their radiance throw
On summer's green and winter's snow,
In such rare splendor that my heart
Would ache from scenes like these to part;
  Though beauties heighten,
  And life-lights brighten,
And joys proceed from every pain,—
I shall not pass this way again.

Then let me pluck the flowers that blow,
And let me listen as I go
  To music rare
  That fills the air;
  And let hereafter
  Songs and laughter
Fill every pause along the way;
And to my spirit let me say:
"O soul, be happy; soon 'tis trod,
The path made thus for thee by God.

Be happy, thou, and bless His name
By whom such marvellous beauty came."
And let no chance by me be lost
To kindness show at any cost.

I shall not pass this way again;
Then let me now relieve some pain,
Remove some barrier from the road,
Or brighten some one's heavy load;
A helping hand to this one lend,
Then turn some other to befriend.

O God, forgive
That now I live
As if I might, sometime, return
To bless the weary ones that yearn
For help and comfort every day,—
For there be such along the way.

O God, forgive that I have seen
The beauty only, have not been
Awake to sorrow such as this;
That I have drunk the cup of bliss
Remembering not that those there be
Who drink the dregs of misery.

I love the beauty of the scene,
Would roam again o'er fields so green;
But since I may not, let me spend
My strength for others to the end,—
For those who tread on rock and stone,
And bear their burdens all alone,
Who loiter not in leafy bowers,
Nor hear the birds nor pluck the flowers.

A larger kindness give to me,
A deeper love and sympathy;
Then, O, one day
May someone say—
Remembering a lessened pain—
"Would she could pass this way again."

Eva Rose York

"I Could Sing Again"

As I was walking along the busy street of my home town today I heard someone singing above the noise of the traffic. It wasn't noisy singing—almost like someone singing to himself—but I heard it. Then I located the singer. He was pushing himself along through the crowd in a wheel chair by the power of his two arms, the only useful limbs he had left. As I caught up with him I said: "A man in a wheel chair singing gives everyone who hears him a lift." He answered: "When I stopped looking at what I had lost, and began looking at all I had left, I could sing again."

Robert E. Bruce

GOLDEN THOUGHTS

Life is made up, not of great sacrifices or duties, but of little things, in which smiles and kindnesses, and small obligations, given habitually, are what win and preserve the heart and secure comfort.

Author Unknown

An ornament of a house is the friends who frequent it.

Ralph Waldo Emerson

A man has made at least a start on discovering the meaning of human life when he plants shade trees under which he knows full well he will never sit.

Author Unknown

If we would build a sure foundation in friendship, we must love our friends for their sakes rather than for our own.

Charlotte Bronte

Golden Nuggets

We don't need soft skies to make friendship a joy to us. What a heavenly thing it is; "World without end," truly. I grow warm thinking of it, and should glow at the thought if all the glaciers of the Alps were heaped over me! Such friends God has given me in this little life of mine!

Celia Thaxter

Don't flatter yourself that friendship authorizes you to say disagreeable things to your intimates. The nearer you come into relation with a person, the more necessary do tact and courtesy become. Except in cases of necessity, which are rare, leave your friend to learn unpleasant things from his enemies; they are ready enough to tell them.

Oliver Wendell Holmes

My coat and I live comfortably together. It has assumed all my wrinkles, does not hurt me anywhere, has moulded itself on my deformities, and is complacent to all my movements, and I only feel its presence because it keeps me warm. Old coats and old friends are the same thing.

Victor Hugo

There are many moments in friendship, as in love, when silence is beyond words. The faults of our friend may be clear to us, but it is well to seem to shut our eyes to them.

Friendship is usually treated by the majority of mankind as a tough and everlasting thing which will survive all manner of bad treatment. But this is an exceedingly great and foolish error; it may die in an hour of a single unwise word.

Marie Louise de la Ramée (Ouida)

If You Have a Friend

If you have a friend worth loving,
  Love him! Yes, and let him know
That you love him, ere life's evening
  Tinge his brow with sunset glow.
Why should good words ne'er be said
Of a friend—till he is dead?

If you hear a prayer that moves you
  By its humble, pleading tone,
Join it! Do not let the seeker
  Bow before God alone.
Why should not your brother share
The strength of "two or three" in prayer?

If you see the hot tears falling
  From a brother's weeping eyes,
Share them! And by kindly sharing
  Own our kinship in the skies.
Why should anyone be glad
When a brother's heart is sad?

If a silvery laugh goes rippling
  Through the sunshine on his face,
Share it! 'Tis the wise man's saying—
  For both grief and joy a place.
There's health and goodness in the mirth
In which an honest laugh has birth.

If your work is made more easy
  By a friendly, helping hand,
Say so! Speak out brave and truly
  Ere the darkness veil the land.
Should a brother workman dear
Falter for a word of cheer?

Scatter thus your seeds of kindness
  All enriching as you go—
Leave them! Trust the Harvest-Giver;
  He will make each seed to grow.
So, until the happy end,
Your life shall never lack a friend.

Anonymous

His Only Request

In olden time there reigned in Persia a great monarch, Shah Abbis, who loved his people. To know them more perfectly he used to mingle with them in various disguises. One day he went as a poor man to the public baths, and there in the tiny cellar he sat beside the fireman who tended the furnace. At mealtime he shared his coarse food and talked to the lonely man as a friend. Again and again he visited him until the man grew to love him. Then one day he told him he was the Emperor and he waited for the man to ask some gift from him. But the fireman sat gazing on him with love and wonder, and at last he spoke: "You left your palace and your glory to sit with me in this dark place, to partake of my coarse fare, to care whether my heart is glad or sorry. On others you may bestow rich presents, but to me you have given yourself; and it only remains to pray that you never withdraw the gift of your friendship."

A sweet word multiplieth friends, and appeaseth enemies, and a gracious tongue in a good man aboundeth.

Be in peace with many, but let one of a thousand be thy counsellor.

If thou wouldst get a friend, try him before thou takest him, and do not credit him easily. . . .

A faithful friend is a strong defense: and he that found him, hath found a treasure. Nothing can be compared to a faithful friend, and no weight of gold and silver is able to countervail the goodness of his fidelity.

Ecclesiasticus I:23

If I Could

If I could know, when each day dies,
I had brought joy to tired eyes;
If I could know, when falls each night,
I'd helped to make some child's life bright;
If I could know, at set of sun,
The fruit of some good deed I'd done;
I'd count my life of grander mold
Than if I'd simply gathered gold.

Edwin Carlile

Friends Are Like Flowers

Friends are like flowers. I have found them so:
The hardy staunch perennials that grow
Year after year are like some friends I know.

One need not cultivate them with great care,
They only need the sun and wind and air
Of trust and love, and they are always there.

Some must be nursed with frequent trowel and spade,
And sheltered from the sun or too much shade,
For fear their frail and clinging bloom may fade.

Friends are like flowers. I would be a friend
Whose blossomings no hand need ever tend:
A perennial on whom hearts can depend.

Grace Noll Crowell

If you are letting miserable misunderstandings run on from year to year, meaning to clear them up someday; if you who are passing men sullenly upon the street, not speaking to them out of some silly spite, and yet knowing that it would fill you with shame and remorse if you heard that one of these men were dead tomorrow morning; if you are letting your neighbor starve, till you hear that he is dying of starvation; or letting your friend's heart ache for a word of appreciation or sympathy, which you mean to give him someday—then if you only could know and see and feel, all of a sudden, that "the time is short," how it would break the spell! How you would go instantly and do the thing which you might never have another chance to do.

Phillips Brooks

He laughed derision when his foes
Against him cast, each man, a stone;
His friend in anger flung a rose —
And all the city heard him moan.

Author Unknown

If thought unlock her mysteries
If Friendship on me smile,
I walk in marble galleries,
I talk with kings the while.

Ralph Waldo Emerson

Easter

Awake

It's morning—glorious Easter morning!

Dawn has flung her myriad shimmering spears deep into the black heart of night, and shattered the smothering shadows.

Silver trumpets of sunrise sound the triumph of light over darkness in crystal clear notes that echo victoriously from the mountain tops, reverberate across plains, and cascade into the depths of green valleys in the old but eternally new paeon of rejoicing:

"Christ is risen! Allelujah!"

They had seemed so utterly hopeless, those two stygian nights when Christ lay in the tomb. The earth shuddered, the rocks broke their hearts at sight of the eternal sacrifice. The millstones of sorrow weighed almost unbearably upon the small band of Christians, their broken hearts still quivering at memory of His suffering, their hopes shattered, their faith subjected to the bitterest test this world has ever known. His pattern of hope had been so different from the one they had woven. They were still too stunned to pick up the raveled threads and weave anew.

Then, the first finger of dawn that pointed to an opened grave!

"Mary."

"Raboni!"

The night is suddenly gone—the stone rolled away from the tomb, never to be replaced!

Life rises, eternally triumphant over death!

Awake and sing praises! It's morning!

The night of weeping is over! Chains are forever broken! Liberty in Christ by the power of the Holy Spirit is bought and paid for by His death and resurrection!

Hallelujah! It's morning!

The Living Christ

A very learned man once said to a little child who believed in the Lord Jesus, "My poor little girl, you don't know whom you believe in. There have been many Christs. In which of them do you believe?"

"I know which One I believe in," replied the child. "I believe in the Christ Who rose from the dead!"

The Meaning of Easter

"I remember this little naked boy just before they killed him. He told me, 'I'm not afraid. It's so terrible here. I'm sure it will be better in heaven.' "

This testimony was given by a survivor of the Nazi concentration camps, where victims were gassed, shot, hanged, drugged, burned alive, and even stomped and kicked to death in World War II.

"I'm sure it will be better in heaven"—this is the universal cry of mankind, particularly in times of great suffering. Even Robert Ingersoll, noted for his unbelief, longed for assurance. At the grave of his brother he said, "In the night of death hope sees a star, and listening love can hear the rustle of a wing."

But do Easter and the resurrection of Christ have meaning only for the future? What about the here and now?

Come to the ancient village of Bethany and stand with Jesus by the tomb of Lazarus, dead four days. Martha, his grief-striken sister, expressed hope that he would live again "at the last day." But her faith did not include "*this day*"—only the "last day."

Martha could see heaven in eternity, but she could not see heaven in time. So Jesus said, "I am the resurrection, and the life" (John 11:25). He did not say "I will be the resurrection" or that "I will give life." He talked about today. He said, "I *am*"—meaning "right now, here, today."

The true meaning of Easter is that eternal life—or heaven—begins as soon as one meets the resurrected Christ. (No, heaven is not here on earth. No, the Christian is not sheltered from the common perils of life such as illness, grief, hunger, cold, pain.) But unless the Christian can show a little bit of heaven in the way he lives here and now, it is doubtful that he would be very comfortable in heaven after death.

A small boy was enjoying his first transcontinental train ride. In the far West the train entered a long, dark tunnel. The boy edged closer to his mother, thinking night had fallen. Then suddenly the train burst into open sunlight. "Look, mother," he cried, "it's tomorrow!"

Have the black tentacles of some night of pain or grief wrapped themselves about you? Do you feel Easter has meaning only for the dim, distant future? Do you feel the here and now is filled with meaningless enigmas? If so, listen again to Jesus' promise, "I am the resurrection." Christ has made tomorrow to dawn on today!

Supreme Court Justice W. O. Douglas' father lay seriously ill. Facing what proved to be a fatal operation, he whispered to his famous son, "If I die it will be glory; if I live it will be grace." To him, Christ was no mysterious, ethereal, ghostlike apparition. He was a living presence in every experience of life as well as death.

This is the meaning of Easter.

Robert J. Hastings

An Early Witness

In the year 94 A.D. Flavius Josephus, a priest of Jerusalem and a court historian who was born in 37 or 38 of the Christian era, published *The Antiquities of the Jews.* The following paragraph from this work gives us a priceless, non-Christian report of Christ and the first Christians.

"Now about this time there was a certain Jesus, a wise man, if indeed he must be called a man. He was in fact the worker of extraordinary things, the teacher of men who accept the truth with pleasure. And he drew to himself many of the Jews and many Greeks also. This man was the Christ. And when Pilate, because the principal men among us denounced him, had punished him on the cross, those who had loved him from the beginning did not cease. In fact, he appeared to them on the third day alive once more, the divine prophets having already spoken these and thousands of other wonderful things concerning him. And even today the tribe of those who from him are called Christians has grown no less."

Flavius Josephus "Antiquities of the Jews"

The Easter Message

Last Easter, when my voice was lifted up
To sing the praises of my Risen Lord,
I had not tasted sorrow's bitter cup,
The music held for me no minor chord.

This Eastertide my stricken heart sends up
The strains I lift in accents clear and strong;
For I have drained the dregs of sorrow's cup,
And learned the meaning of the Easter song.

I know the sweetness of the minor chord,
The glory of the major full and clear,
I know the power of my Risen Lord,—
He lives, and they shall live whom I hold dear.

And though I cannot help the tears that flow,
And though my heart is sad as heart can be
I sing the Easter song because I know
The blessed Easter message is for me.

Author Unknown

Resurgence

Out of the earth, the rose,
  Out of the night, the dawn:
Out of my heart, with all its woes,
  High courage to press on.

Laura Lee Randall

Spring

Now fades the last long streak of snow,
  Now burgeons every maze of quick
  About the flowering squares, and thick
By ashen roots the violets blow.

Now rings the woodland loud and long,
  The distance takes a lovelier hue,
  And drowned in yonder living blue
The lark becomes a sightless song.

Now dance the lights on lawn and lea,
  The flocks are whiter down the vale,
  And milkier every milky sail,
On winding stream or distant sea;

Where now the seamew pipes, or dives
  In yonder greening gleam, and fly
  The happy birds, that change their sky
To build and brood, that live their lives.

From land to land; and in my breast
  Spring wakens too; and my regret
  Becomes an April violet,
And buds and blossoms like the rest.

Alfred Tennyson

What Easter Means to Me

Easter season, and suddenly the whole world seems to be accented with soft pastel hues and shafts of sunlight and bright spring hopes.

But I hold a book in my hands, and remember . . .

I see a village in Viet Nam, a little village called Hiep Duc. A place that was and is no more.

I remember the homes that lay in ashes and the little boy whose tiny shoulder shook at the sound of gunfire, but whose face was an expressionless mask of shock.

And I remember how, as the battle raged and the shots crackled and the mortars thumped, a young Vietnamese soldier crumpled bullet-riddled at the edge of the jungle.

With other combat correspondents and some of his fellow soldiers I ran to his side. We carried him into the one shell of a building which was left . . . and then stood by—helpless—as he died before our eyes.

And when he had died, I walked out into the open sunlight and looked around. On all sides were the silver jets, sweeping down to bomb or strafe or fire their rockets.

Five feet away lay bodies still in death. I winced as I remembered the gentle features of the young soldier, hardly more than a boy, who had just died at my feet.

I had come to Hiep Duc with a strange feeling of compulsion, even though I had known the helicopter was carrying me into the blood and stench and death and heartache of a battlefield.

I looked up into the deep blue sky overhead. "All right, Father," I asked, "Why? Why have You brought me here?"

And then I saw it—this book I now hold in my hand. This book which is The Book—a Vietnamese New Testament.

I do not read Vietnamese, but I saw the heading: "Mac." *Mac*—Mark. The Gospel of St. Mark!

My eyes moved to the big number 16. Mark, the sixteenth chapter.

I had my answer. I knew why I had come. For Mark 16 is the story of the Resurrection!

Nearby, death. Apparently the owner of the Testament also had lost his life. But perhaps, just before death came, he saw it: Mac 16. And perhaps he heard a familiar Voice say: "I am the Resurrection and the Life. He that believeth on Me though he were dead, *yet shall he live*!"

So I hold this Book-more-than-a-book in my hand. Because I do, because I remember Hiep Duc, Easter means more to me now.

What does it mean? It means life in the midst of death; hope in the midst of heartache. For I remember those words in Vietnamese.

Chua Jesus Song Lai—"Jesus Christ rises from the dead!"

Larry Ward

He Is Risen

I was standing before the window of an art store, where a picture of the Crucifixion of our Lord was on exhibition. As I gazed I was conscious of the approach of another, and turning, beheld a little lad gazing intently at this picture also. Noticing that this mite of humanity was a sort of street arab, I thought I would speak to him; so I asked, pointing to the picture, "Do you know who it is?" "Yes," came the quick response, "that's our Saviour," with a mingled look of pity and surprise that I should not know what the picture represented. With an evident desire to enlighten me further, he continued, after a pause: "Them's the soldiers, the Roman soldiers, and," with a long-drawn sigh, "that woman crying there is His mother."

He waited, apparently for me to question him further, then thrust his hands into his pockets, and with a reverent and subdued voice added, "They killed Him, mister. Yes, sir, they killed Him." I looked at the little, dirty, ragged fellow, and asked, "Where did you learn this?" He replied, "At the Mission Sunday School."

Full of thoughts regarding the benefits of Mission Sunday Schools, I turned away and resumed my walk, leaving the little lad still looking at the picture. I had not walked a block when I heard his childish treble calling, "Mister! say, mister!" I turned. He was running toward me, but paused; then up went his little hand, and with a triumphant sound in his voice he said: *"I wanted to tell you He rose again!"*

Author Unknown

His Garment's Hem

O Blessed Lord, I stoop to Thy flowing garment,
I reach a timid hand to touch its hem
Here among the throng that is surging, pressing
Close about Thee, and I the humblest of them.
Then lo, He speaks, and His voice is kind and gentle:
"Who in this throng has touched me?" questions He;
And I, who have been needing it so, move forward
To receive the wondrous gift He is giving me:
The gift of healing for body, mind and spirit,
The gift of virtue from His own life to mine,
And He speaks the blessed words of commendation:
"Thy faith hath made thee whole." O words that shine
Like silver light to pierce the clouding darkness,
Humbly, indeed, I bow before that praise.
Grant me, O blessed One, the strength to follow
Thee closer—with greater faith throughout my days.

Grace Noll Crowell

Look Up

Look up, O heart; and then, O heart, kneel down
In humble adoration: give no crown
Nor golden diadem to your fair Lord,
But offer love and beauty by your word.

Let your faith burn, O heart: and let your eyes
Shine with such joy where deepest night still lies
In some too tired and over-burdened mind:
Let Christ be seen, wherever you are kind.

O heart, let your light shine so that all men
May see your works and glorify again
Your Father: and oh! let your light be gay,
And full of quiet laughter all the day.

The everlasting fire of love, O heart,
Has blazed in you and it will not depart.
Wherefore, O heart, exult and praises sing:
Lift up your voice and make the echoes ring.

Raise up your hands, O heart: your fingers raise
In adoration; and in bursting praise
Sing all your songs of beauty with delight,
You larks, exulting in the summer light.

O heart, rise up: O heart be lifted high.
Rejoice; for Light was slain to-day, yet did not die.

Anonymous

The Empty Tomb

Most tombs are dear to our humanity because of what they contain. I go to Grant's tomb on Riverside Drive. Why do I stand uncovered? Because I remember that the body of a patriot rests there. I stand by the slab marking Livingstone's grave in Westminster Abbey. Why the beating heart and the moistened eye? I remember that here lies as heroic dust as was ever organized into a human body. And so it is with the graves of father, mother, sister, brother, husband, wife, lover, friend, throughout the wide world. Their entombed dust hallows the place of their entombment. We prize it for what it contains. But one tomb has imperishable glory because of its emptiness. It is the tomb of Christ visited by the Marys and made empty by a miraculous act of Almighty God.

Frederick F. Shannon

There's a Light Upon the Mountains

There's a light upon the mountains,
And the day is at the spring,
When our eyes shall see the beauty
And the glory of the King:
Weary was our heart with waiting,
And the night-watch seemed so long,
But His triumph-day is breaking,
And we hail it with a song.

In the fading of the starlight
We may see the coming morn;
And the lights of men are paling
In the splendors of the dawn;
For the eastern skies are glowing
As with light of hidden fire,
And the hearts of men are stirring
With the throbs of deep desire.

He is breaking down the barriers,
He is casting up the way;
He is calling for His angels
To build up the gates of day:
But His angels here are human,
Not the shining hosts above;
For the drum-beats of His army
Are the heart-beats of our love.

Hark! we hear a distant music,
And it comes with fuller swell;
'Tis the triumph-song of Jesus,
Of our King, Immanuel!
Go ye forth with joy to meet Him!
And, my soul, be swift to bring
All thy sweetest and thy dearest
For the triumph of our King!

Henry Burton

Golden Nuggets

If Spring came but once in a century, instead of once a year, or burst forth with the sound of an earthquake, and not in silence, what wonder and expectation there would be in all hearts to behold the miraculous change!

Henry Wadsworth Longfellow

There are persons so radiant, so genial, so kind, so pleasure-bearing, that you instinctively feel in their presence that they do you good; whose coming into a room is like the bringing of a lamp there.

Henry Ward Beecher

As long as love flourishes in the center of your heart you are young. So long as you radiate beauty, hope, cheer, courage to your fellowmen, so long you are young.

The continuity of life is never broken; the river flows onward and is lost to our sight; but under its new horizon it carries the same waters which it gathered under ours, and its unseen valleys are made glad by the offerings which are borne down to them from the past,—flowers, perchance, the germs of which its own waves had planted on the banks of Time.

Whittier

There is a cathedral in Europe with an organ at each end. Organ answers organ, and the music waves backward and forward with indescribable effect. The time will come when heaven and earth will be but different parts of one great accord. It will be joy here and joy there, Jesus here and Jesus there. Organ to organ. Hallelujah to Hallelujah.

T. DeWitt Talmage

After the Storm

I do not know where I get that feeling; but as I read this connected history, it seems to me as though the crucifixion were like one of those summer thunderstorms that we have, in which all the heavens appear to be full of darkness, and conflict, and turmoil. The terrible thunder-cracks that roll through the darkness; the great striving winds that now tug at the trees which groan under their hands, and that now beat on the house; the hissing rain; all the wild commotion of the elements—these fill the soul full of imaginations and strange terrors. And yet we sleep (I used to, as a child), and wake, and sleep; and when the morning comes, there is not a cloud in the air. It is as if the heavens were one vast bowl, or goblet, filled with the wine of life; and the sun seems steeping the very heavens. Not a leaf moves except when a drop of water falls from it and changes its equipoise. And all the birds sing, and all voices seem jubilant, and all the earth seems refreshed and more beautiful. And so it affects me when I read of the tumult of the crucifixion on Calvary, and the after quiet.

For then, there are the scenes of the garden—the ministration of angels; the sweet surprise of the different groups that came to the sepulchre. It is all tranquil. It is all joyful. Previous to that event there had been tumult, from the time of Christ's appearance on the earth; but when once He has passed the portals of the tomb; when once He has come forth from the sepulchre, it is all serene; it is all sweet. It is as it should be. Now we can see it. The Saviour has risen; and all the signs and tokens of His presence are gladness and radiance and peace.

Henry Ward Beecher

The Cross and the Tomb

"He died," saith the cross, "my very name
  Was a hated thing and a word of shame;
But since Christ hung on my arms outspread,
  With nails in His hands and thorns on His head,
They do but measure—set high, flung wide—
  The measureless love of the Crucified."
"He rose," said the tomb, "I was dark and drear,
  And the sound of my name wove a spell of fear;
But the Lord of Life in my depths hath lain
  To break Death's power and rend his chain;
And a light streams forth from my open door,
  For the Lord is risen; He dies no more."

Annie Johnson Flint

Easter

Easter is *the soul's great power house.* Even for my little lamp of life, I need the pulsing light waves of immortality. The filament of my soul may be fragile, but it commands qualitative, if not quantitative, energy from a divine dynamo. Mortality cannot be illuminated by its own devices. Not even Joseph's tomb would have a message for us today unless it had been burst open from within by "the power of His resurrection." That power is, too, much more than mystical; it is moral. It makes our enfeebled wills mighty. It causes the dominant energies of our spirits to break forth into action. It gives meaning to daily struggle, for it exposes one to the irresistible tides of eternity. When one's life is linked to the resurrection of Christ, he becomes invincible and victorious.

This glorious day has also become to me the propulsion of a great task. It set my heart aglow and my hands to work. It provides apprenticeship at first and then calls me to higher and more capacious rooms of service. Easter glorifies unselfish toil for it guarantees the indestructibility of love. It helps me to discriminate between the second rate and the best. It puts a premium upon people, not things. It helps me to pray, "Thy kingdom come," and then go forth to bring it in.

Easter is God's bottle for my tears. It is the perpetual source of consolation. Of what avail would Jesus' words, "Let not your heart be troubled," have been if God had not raised Him from the dead? How could I face the ruthless severing of ties of affection at the hands of death had I not confidence in the One who lives beyond this dying, and who shall bring with Him in glory those who have fallen asleep? Who other than the risen Saviour can comfort us?

And Easter means that *the hallmark of divine redemption has been stamped upon personality.* Man was not created for the ash heap. "Dust thou art to dust returneth was not spoken of the soul." "God did not permit His Holy One to see corruption." He has given me an inimitable pledge of His word, in my heart and conscience and most clearly in His risen Son, that because He lives I shall live also, that where He is there shall I be, and that "I shall be like Him for I shall see Him as He is."

William Hiram Foulkes

The Message of Easter

Next to the celebration of Christmas, no other celebration is so inspiring as that of Easter, commemorating the Resurrection of Christ, and it is so apt to be celebrated when all Nature has its awakening to newness of life. Symbolic is the beautiful white Easter lily.

There had to be a Resurrection to fulfill the promise of prophecy and to give emphasis to the inspired message of Christ's ministry among men as to eternal life. There were skeptics among His followers who found it difficult to believe that Christ had risen from the dead, but when He showed them the wounds in His hands and feet, they believed.

It was then that Jesus told His followers to go into all the world and preach the gospel and to do the things that He did in His name. It was soon after His Resurrection that He uttered those beautiful words: "Lo, I am with you always, even unto the end of the world."

Easter is a challenge to the faith of us all. It should be a time of renewal of this faith. Everything during this springtime is an example of renewal. There is continuity in nature. It should be attached to our faith as well. Easter flashes its light about us and gives to us a new vision of hope and confidence.

Had the Resurrection taken place in our day, the newspapers would have flashed around the world those familiar words: "Christ is risen!" Those words are just as meaningful today. There is assurance to them. Just the same as there is assurance that the bare trees of winter will be transformed in the springtime with the beautiful foliage of former years and the lilies with their perfect blooms.

The message of Easter is one of immortality. There is a purpose to everything. All growth is a manifestation of the divine will in all life. Scattered all over this earth are flowers of every description, perfect in design, and each with its appointive courage. Each exemplifying a Resurrection.

George Matthew Adams

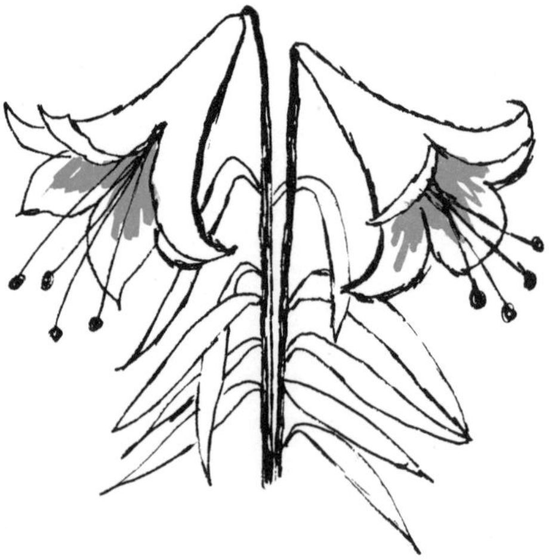

Golden Prayers

Into Thy hands, O God, we commend ourselves, and all who are dear to us, this day. Let the gift of Thy special presence be with us even to its close. Grant us never to lose sight of Thee all the day long, but to worship, and pray to Thee, that at eventide we may again give thanks unto Thee. AMEN.

O Lord, our heavenly Father, who orderest all things for our eternal good, mercifully enlighten our minds, and give us a firm and abiding trust in Thy love and care. Silence our murmurings, quiet our fears, and dispel our doubts, that, rising above our afflictions and our anxieties, we may rest on Thee, the Rock of everlasting Strength. AMEN.

"After the Winter... God Sends the Spring"

Easter is a season
Of hope and joy and cheer,
There's beauty all around us
To see and touch and hear . . .
So, no matter how downhearted
And discouraged we may be,
New hope is born when we behold
Leaves budding on a tree . . .
Or when we see a timid flower
Push through the frozen sod
And open wide in glad surprise
Its petaled eyes to God . . .
For this is just God saying—
"Lift up your eyes to Me,
And the bleakness of your spirit,
Like the budding springtime tree,
Will lose its wintry darkness
And your heavy heart will sing"—
For God never sends the winter
Without the joy of spring.

Helen Steiner Rice

I Saw the Place Where the Lord Lay

It has been my high privilege to visit the Bible Lands nine times during the past fifteen years and these opportunities to come to a finer understanding of the geographical background of the Biblical record have been most inspiring and rewarding.

It is difficult to describe adequately the emotions which filled my heart as I set foot upon the highways, Bible in hand, where my blessed Lord had also walked and viewed the scenes upon which His eyes had rested daily for the thirty-three years of His life among men. Palestine is a living, up-to-date commentary on the Old and New Testaments, and the places and personalities of the sacred inspired story become vividly real.

There is so much that one feels just must be seen and which even these repeated visits have hardly begun to exhaust. For example, it was not until my seventh tour that I stood on Mount Nebo over against Jericho and saw for myself all the promised land even as millenia before, the Lord had shown it to His servant Moses. Now, we would not think of returning without planning to stand again on those same heights for a renewed vision.

I went from the shepherds' fields to Bethlehem and the Church of the Nativity. I stood by Mary's well in Nazareth, Christ's boyhood home. In Cana, I saw the place of His first miracle. At Bethany, I relived the precious times Jesus had with His friends, Mary, Martha and Lazarus. It was a thrill to sit by Jacob's well at Sychar and rehearse the conversation He had with the Samaritan woman as she received from him the water of life. I rode a boat on the waters of Galilee and walked its shores to the site of the Sermon on the Mount, that of the feeding of the five thousand, and then the synagogue at Capernaum where He preached.

But the two historic places which made the deepest impression on my heart and soul were Golgotha where He was crucified and the Garden Tomb where they laid the body of the Lord. I am glad that the English Committee which has responsibility for the care of these two sacred sites has not made shrines of them, but rather preserved them as far as possible in their original rugged state.

The Place Called Calvary

In English, it is "skull," in Greek, "Calvary," in Hebrew, "Golgotha." Whatever language is used, it was a dreadful place of death, outside the walls of Jerusalem.

I climbed to the top of the north wall, east of the Damascus Gate, and there it was! A hush fell upon my heart. The top was bare, smooth, scalp-like. Below were deep cavities clearly resembling eyes, a nose and a mouth.

This grim place is where Christ was lifted up between heaven and earth, as the atoning Sacrifice for the sins of the whole world. Overlooked by a large part of the city, almost in the form of a semi-circle, it was somewhat like a Roman amphitheatre. How easily *"those that passed by"* could witness the crucifixion scene.

As I looked at it, I thought of my own sin and the part it, too, had in nailing Him to that Cross, and I thanked Him again for dying in my room and stead, to provide my eternal salvation.

The Garden Tomb

Just to the left of Calvary, and much below its level is a beautiful garden fragrant with zinnias, asters, petunias and rosemary, growing beneath old trees. In this garden is a tomb. It seems that here the words of John 19:41 are corroborated: *"Now in the place where He was crucified, there was a garden, and in the garden a new sepulchre, wherein was never man yet laid."*

As I approached the ancient garden at the foot of the hill, a huge door opened to admit me. Awe filled my heart as I walked over to the Garden Tomb, and stooped to enter the low door even as the disciples had on that first Easter morning.

Inside are two compartments, separated by a low limestone wall. The outer room where I stood is about seven by ten feet with a seven and a half foot ceiling. I looked over the wall into the second room where there is a crypt about seven feet long and two wide.

At the far end is a rounded depression for the head of a person to rest. This may well be the place where on the day of the resurrection *"two angels in white were sitting, the one at the head and the other at the feet where the body of Jesus had lain."*

As I had thought about the death of my Lord on Calvary, so now my mind and heart were concerned with the resurrection. I walked about the tomb, seated myself on the ledge where perhaps a white-robed angel had once sat, and considered the "infallible proofs": the fearful earthquake, the terrified guards, the broken Roman seal, the removed stone, the frightened women, the orderly grave clothes, the angel visitants, the dumbfounded disciples, the manifest lies of the enemies of Christ who *"gave large money unto the soldiers, saying, Say ye, His disciples came by night and stole Him away while we slept,"* and the seventeen personal appearances which Jesus made after His resurrection, including the one where "He was seen of above five hundred brethren at once." God so multiplied the evidence that the resurrection of Christ is one of the best attested facts of history.

So I rejoiced that day as I saw where the Lord lay, that this is indeed an *empty* tomb; that we do not worship One still hanging on a cross or lying in a sepulchre. He is a *living* Saviour, waiting to forgive and transform us and prepare us to live with Him forever. Nothing is as important as this matter of our individual relationship to God.

J. Palmer Muntz

April Rise

If I ever saw blessing in the air
I see it now in this still early day
Where lemon-green the vaporous morning drips
Wet sunlight on the powder of my eye.

Blown bubble-film of blue, the sky wraps 'round
Weeds of warm light whose every root and rod
Splutters with soapy green, and all the world
Sweats with the bead of summer in its bud.

If ever I heard blessing it is there
Where birds in trees that shoals and shadows are
Splash with their hidden wings and drops of sound
Break on my ears their crests of throbbing air.

Pure in the haze the emerald sun dilates,
The lips of sparrows milk the mossy stones,
While white as water by the lake a girl
Swims her green hand among the gathered swans.

Now, as the almond burns its smoking wick,
Dropping small flames to light the candled grass;
Now, as my low blood scales its second chance,
If ever world were blessed, now it is.

Laurie Lee

All Things Bright and Beautiful

All things bright and beautiful,
All creatures great and small,
All things wise and wonderful,
The Lord God made them all.

He gave us eyes to see them,
And lips that we might tell
How great is God Almighty
Who has made all things well.

Cecil Frances Alexander

Home and Family

I Remember

I remember summer and the farm—the softness of the little chick in my palm—the way it tickled when the tiny furry ball moved.
I remember the trees dancing and the bushes nodding and the blades of grass bending as I rolled down and down the hill, over and over.
And the great Indian's head, and the airplane, and the mountains in the sky, and how, when I closed my eyes halfway, I could make them move.
And the feel of the hay down my shirt when I jumped from the loft; the smell of the silo, and hiding in a tree as my sister called and called.
And chasing the ducks and the geese and the cow—through the flowers, across the fields, over the hill, faster and faster, and laughing as I ran!
I remember how it was, and, remembering, I am happy. This is my Father's world, and it is good. Indeed, it *is* very good.

Dina Donohue

Folks Need a Lot of Loving

Folks need a lot of loving in the morning;
The day is all ahead, with cares beset—
The cares we know, and those that give no warning;
For love is God's own antidote for fret.

Folks need a heap of loving at the noontime—
The battle lull, the moment snatched from strife—
Halfway between the waking and the croontime,
When bickering and worriment are rife.

Folks hunger so for loving at the nighttime,
When wearily they take them home to rest—
At slumber song and turning-out-the-light time.
Of all the times for loving, that's the best.

Folks want a lot of loving every minute—
The sympathy of others and their smile!
Till life's end, from the moment they begin it,
Folks need a lot of loving all the while.

Strickland Gillilan

Dearly Beloved

Mark Twain dearly loved his wife "Livy" and continued to court her during their entire married life. He often wrote little notes to be put on her dresser, or on her breakfast tray. Whenever they were separated he wrote love letters to her every day. On November 27, 1885, the seventeenth anniversary of their engagement and her fortieth birthday he wrote her the following letter:

"We have reached another milestone, my darling, and a very, very remote one from the place whence we started; but we look back over a pleasant landscape—valleys that are still green, plains that still bear flowers, hills that still sleep in the soft light of that far morning of blessed memory. And here we have company on the journey—ah, such precious company, such inspiring, such lovely, and gracious company! and how they lighten the march! Our faces are toward the sunset, now, but these are with us, to hold our hands, and stay our feet, and while they abide, and our old love grows and never diminishes, our march shall still be through flowers and green fields, and the evening light as pleasant as that old soft morning glow yonder behind.

Your Husband"

The Love Letters of Mark Twain

The One Hundred and Twenty-seventh Psalm

Except the Lord build the house,
they labour in vain that build it:
except the Lord keep the city,
the watchman waketh but in vain.

It is vain for you to rise up early,
to sit up late,
to eat the bread of sorrows:
for so he giveth his beloved sleep.

Lo, children are an heritage of the Lord:
and the fruit of the womb is his reward.

As arrows are in the hand of a mighty man:
so are the children of youth.

Happy is the man that hath his quiver full of them;
they shall not be ashamed:
but they shall speak with the enemies in the gate.

A Mother's Last Letter to Her Son

Tragedy marred the early life of Andrew Jackson. Before he was born his father died. Before he was ten years old, prison fever took the life of his mother who was attending American soldiers during the Revolutionary War. Then his two brothers died in the service of their country. At the age of 14 he was an orphan and without any family.

Andrew did have a heritage, however—a letter from his mother giving him some good advice. It was the last letter she ever wrote him, and it read:

Dear Andrew:

If I should not see you again I wish you to remember and treasure up some things I have already said to you: in this world you will have to make your own way. To do that you must have friends. You can make friends by being honest, and you can keep them by being steadfast. You must keep in mind that friends worth having will on the long run expect as much from you as they give to you.

To forget an obligation or be ungrateful for a kindness is a base crime. Men guilty of this crime sooner or later must suffer the penalty.

In personal conduct always be polite, but never obsequious. No one will respect you more than you esteem yourself. Avoid quarrels as long as you can without yielding to imposition. But sustain your manhood always . . .

Never wound the feelings of others. If ever you have to vindicate your feelings or defend your honor, do it calmly. If angry at first, wait till your wrath cools before you proceed.

Love,

Mother

The Joy of Work

Give us, oh, give us, the man who sings at his work! He will do more in the same time,—he will do it better,—he will persevere longer. One is scarcely sensible of fatigue whilst he marches to music. The very stars are said to make harmony as they revolve in their spheres. Wondrous is the strength of cheerfulness, altogether past calculation in its powers of endurance. Efforts, to be permanently useful, must be uniformly joyous, a spirit all sunshine, graceful from very gladness, beautiful because bright.

Thomas Carlyle

golden prayers

The day returns and brings us the petty round of irritating concerns and duties. Help us to play the man, help us to perform them with laughter and kind faces, let cheerfulness abound with industry. Give us to go blithely on our business all this day, bring us to our resting beds weary and content and undishonored, and grant us in the end the gift of sleep.

Robert Louis Stevenson

golden nuggets

Thank God every morning when you get up that you have something to do that day which must be done, whether you like it or not. Being forced to work and forced to do your best will breed in you temperance and self-control, diligence and strength of will, cheerfulness and content, and a hundred virtues which the idle never know.

Charles Kingsley

Home . . . there's no place like it . . . Tomorrow will have its problems and anxieties, but tonight the heart-strings are entwined with garlands of quiet peace. Does wealth, power, or title bestow a sweeter gift?

Anonymous

The father and mother of an unnoticed family who, in their seclusion, awaken the mind of one child to the idea and love of goodness, who awaken in him a strength of will to repel temptation, and who send him out prepared to profit by the conflicts of life, surpass in influence a Napoleon breaking the world to his sway.

William Ellery Channing

Golden Years

Mothers Never Change

Not long ago when an allergy forced me to take a month from my work as a singer with the Billy Graham Crusades, it gave me the chance to visit my 84-year-old mother back in Syracuse, New York.

One night about 3 a.m. I woke up coughing. I tried to muffle the sound to keep from waking her, but in a minute or two I heard her fumbling for her slippers.

Mothers don't change; the same instinct which had her on her feet at a whimper from one of her eight babies was getting her out of bed now.

A few minutes later there was a rap on my door and in she came with a cup of hot tea and a plate of her own oatmeal cookies. Except for the white hair framing her face, it might have been 50 years before.

Both of us were remembering an earlier illness when I was between 10 and 12 years old, a mysterious infection which kept me out of school nearly two years—and turned an already shy boy into a monument of self-consciousness.

Big for my age anyway, when I went back to school and was placed in a room with boys and girls two years younger than I was, I wanted to sink through the floor.

The few times when I had to speak in public were agony.

The problem persisted even after I left home.

Once in Chicago I was trapped into giving a talk. Wistfully I thought of my father's warm, wise, seemingless effortless sermons back home. As a preacher, Dad always had been as fluent as I was tongue-tied.

And then inspiration came. What if Dad were to outline a talk for me! I wrote giving him the subject and begging him to suggest some good points.

Dad's reply didn't fill a third of the space on a penny postcard: "Son, God helped Baalam's donkey to talk so I'm sure He can do something for you. Love, Dad."

But although Dad would never do for me what I could do for myself, it was he and Mother who helped me at last to move beyond the shyness that would have robbed my life of any chance for service.

As Mother and I talked that night, the past seemed very close. And I found myself recalling other objects that her love and Dad's had endowed with special meaning for me.

The first was a piano. The Shea family had no need for an alarm clock; our day started with Mother singing at the piano.

In singing I found a release from the old problem of bashfulness. As I grew older, I poured out in song thoughts and feelings I had no other way to express.

The final vignette focused on a straight-back chair. It was the chair in which my father sat the night he delivered his final sermon at Willett Memorial Church in Syracuse.

At age 73, cancer had ravished his body and left him too weak to climb into the pulpit.

Though Dad's body was weakened, his spirit was never stronger. His sermon was one of great reassurance. In a sense, his words were much the same as those we found in a note beside his bed after he had gone.

"Life has been wonderful," he wrote, "the promises of God precious, the eternal hope glorious."

I placed the empty teacup on the nightstand.

"Can I give you something more?" she said.

She meant tea, but my thoughts were still on those other things. A piano, a straight-back chair—music, God and hope eternal.

"Thank you, Mother," I said. "You've given me everything I need."

George Beverly Shea

Bless This House

Bless this house, O Lord, we pray,
Make it safe by night and day;
Bless these walls, so firm and stout,
Keeping want and trouble out;
Bless the roof and chimneys tall,
Let thy peace lie over all;
Bless this door, that it may prove
Ever open to joy and love.

Helen Taylor

Dirt Farmer

He finds beauty among these simple things;
The path a plow makes in the rich, red loam,
Gay sun-gold in ripe wheat—a plover's wings—
A cow-bell, tinkling as the herd comes home.
He treads the soil, with earth-love in his heart;
Watches the young crops spring from fertile ground,
Loves the warm rain that makes the peach buds start,
Land—and a man—in close communion bound!

Arden Antony

The Most Beautiful Thing

An artist who wanted to paint the most beautiful picture in the world, asked a pastor "What is the most beautiful thing?"

"Faith," said the parson; "you find it at every altar."

The artist asked a young bride the same question. "Love," she replied. "Love builds poverty into riches; sweetens tears; makes much of little. Without it there is no beauty."

A weary soldier told him: "Peace is the most beautiful thing in the world. War is the most ugly. Wherever you find peace, you find beauty."

"Faith, Love, and Peace! How can I paint them?" thought the artist. Entering his door, he saw Faith in the eyes of his children and Love in the eyes of his wife. And there in his own home the artist saw the Peace that Love and Faith had built.

So he painted the picture of "the most beautiful thing in the world." And he called it, "Home."

In Thine Arms

Our families in Thine arms enfold
As Thou didst keep Thy folk of old.

Oliver Wendell Holmes

Better Than Gold

Better than grandeur, better than gold,
Than rank and titles a thousandfold,
Is a healthy body and a mind at ease,
And simple pleasures that always please.
A heart that can feel for another's woe,
And share his joys with a genial glow;
With sympathies large enough to enfold
All men as brothers, is better than gold.

Better than gold is a peaceful home
Where all the fireside characters come,
The shrine of love, the heaven of life,
Hallowed by mother, or sister, or wife.
However humble the home may be,
Or tried with sorrow by heaven's decree,
The blessings that never were bought or sold,
And center there, are better than gold.

Abram Joseph Ryan

GOLDEN NOTES

A Tribute to Home

It's lovely in Long Island in October. The trees are a brilliant red and gold; and in East Hampton, where John Howard Payne spent much of his boyhood, there was a crisp tang of the sea in the air.

But this was *Paris,* not Long Island. This was Paris, on a dull, gray day in October, in the year 1822. John Payne was far from family and friends, far from the rambler-covered cottage in East Hampton, the old homestead he remembered so well from his childhood . . . and had always loved. He had been living abroad now for nine years. As an actor and playwright he had been busy, successful, and in some ways happier than he had been at home. But he had always been lonely.

In his room on the upper floor of a lodginghouse near the Palais Royale, Payne stood at the window and looked down at the happy, hurrying crowds in the streets below.

People laughed, and waved, and greeted each other, and hurried on . . . to their homes, their families, their loved ones. . . . Only *he* had nowhere to go but this lonely room! He was suddenly homesick—completely, unutterably homesick.

He turned impatiently from the window. He had no time to stand mooning about the past, dreaming about East Hampton. But the mood and the memories stayed with him, sat at his elbow as he wrote, filled his heart and mind so completely he could think of nothing else. *Home!* What strange, compelling magic that simple word possessed! How it brought memories rushing back, joyous and comforting, memories of family and fireside, of pleasures long since past. . . .

He began writing the words of "Home, Sweet Home." And into it he poured all his own aching loneliness, all his longing for the sights and scenes of his boyhood.

In the early part of 1823, John Payne sold three plays. One of these was *Clari, or, the Maid of Milan;* and in the first scene Payne had introduced the song he called "Home, Sweet Home."

Clari opened in Covent Garden Theatre on May 8, 1823. The title role was played by Maria Tree. As she stepped to the center of the stage and began to sing, the audience—restless and even unruly up to that point—was suddenly silent. The singer's own voice choked up as she sang, her eyes filled with tears, and by the time she reached the end of the song there wasn't a dry eye in the audience. The tender words, the plaintive melody, had tremendous appeal . . . and the song was an instant, an overwhelming success.

It was heard everywhere. Singers lavished their art on it. Ships' bands played it as they left port. Mothers crooned it to their babies. Choirs sang it in churches and schools. Even prisoners sang it in their cells, pouring out their souls in the song that characterized the family fireside and home and promising themselves to live worthier lives.

Years later, Jenny Lind, "the Swedish Nightingale," sang in Washington for one of the most distinguished audiences ever seen in a concert hall in the United States. At the end of the concert, she smiled, then turned to face a gentle, white-haired man seated obscurely in the audience. It was John Howard Payne, now nearly sixty years old. Without taking her eyes from his face, Jenny Lind sang "Home, Sweet Home." The vast audience was electrified; all eyes were turned toward Payne, who was completely overcome by the tribute. As Jenny Lind sang his famous song, he wept openly. And there were many in that great audience who wept with him—profoundly moved, as people always were, by the emotional impact of his song.

Payne died eighteen months later, his enduring fame assured. "Home, Sweet Home" has been translated into every language, sung in almost every land, known and loved by millions of people for more than a century. Its influence will continue as long as people love their homes and cherish their family ties.

Home, Sweet Home

'Mid pleasures and palaces though we may roam,
Be it ever so humble, there's no place like home;
A charm from the sky seems to hallow us there,
Which, seek through the world, is ne'er met with elsewhere.
  Home, home, sweet, sweet home!
There's no place like home, there's no place like home!

An exile from home, splendor dazzles in vain;
Oh, give me my lowly thatched cottage again!
The birds singing gaily, that came at my call—
Give me them—and the peace of mind, dearer than all!
  Home, home, sweet, sweet home!
There's no place like home, there's no place like home!

How sweet 'tis to sit 'neath a fond father's smile,
And the cares of a mother to soothe and beguile!
Let others delight 'mid new pleasures to roam,
But give me, oh, give me, the pleasures of home,
  Home, home, sweet, sweet home!
There's no place like home, there's no place like home!

To thee I'll return, overburdened with care;
The heart's dearest solace will smile on me there;
No more from that cottage again will I roam;
Be it ever so humble, there's no place like home.
  Home, home, sweet, sweet home!
There's no place like home, there's no place like home!

Sanctuary

This is our Place.

A flowered shrine within a friendly town
Where one can lose the world and be at peace
Beneath the trees, or pottering in the sun—
Or watch the pageantry of fiery fleece
Against the skyline when the day is done.
A modest plot, but one we call our own—
This is our Place.

This is our House.

Together, we have dreamed it into being—
Watched o'er its building till it stood at last
Smiling in welcome, perfect in our sight.
It took us to its hearth and held us fast
To guard our life and love by day and night—
Safe haven now and far beyond our seeing—
This is our House.

This is our Home.

No other place can ever hold, for me,
The garnered treasure of these fruitful years—
That you and I, my dear, are living through.
Whether they bring us joy or pain and tears
Within these walls I share it all with you
And catch an echo of God's symphony.
This is our Home!

R. K. Fletcher

Your Place

Is your place a small place?
Tend it with care!—
He set you there.

Whate'er your place, it is
Not yours alone, but His
Who set you there.

John Oxenham

The Sisters

The waves forever move;
The hills forever rest:
Yet each the heavens approve,
And Love alike hath blessed
A Martha's household care,
A Mary's cloistered prayer.

John Banister Tabb

A Country Home

I visited a country home: a modest, quiet house sheltered by great trees and set in a circle of field and meadow, gracious with the promise of harvest. Barns and cribs were filled, and the old smokehouse odorous with treasure; the fragrance of pink and hollyhock mingling with the aroma of garden and orchard, and resonant with the hum of bees and the poultry's busy clucking; inside the house, thrift, comfort, and that cleanliness that is next to godliness; the restful beds, the open fireplace, the books and papers, and the old clock that had held its steadfast pace amid the frolic of weddings, that had welcomed in steady measure the new-born babes of the family, and kept company with the watchers of the sick-bed, and had ticked the solemn requiem of the dead; and the well-worn Bible that, thumbed by fingers long since stilled, and blurred with tears of eyes long since closed, held the simple annals of the family, and the heart and conscience of the home.

Henry W. Grady

A Prayer for a Little Home

God send us a little home
To come back to when we roam—
Low walls and fluted tiles,
Wide windows, a view for miles;
Red firelight and deep chairs;
Small white beds upstairs;
Great talk in little nooks;
Dim colors, rows of books;
One picture on each wall;
Not many things at all.

God send us a little ground—
Tall trees standing round,
Homely flowers in brown sod,
Overhead, the stars, O God!
God bless, when winds blow,
Our home and all we know.

Florence Bone

They Might Not Need Me; But They Might

They might not need me; but they might.
I'll let my head be just in sight;
A smile as small as mine might be
Precisely their necessity.

Emily Dickinson

GOLDEN THOUGHTS

A good laugh is sunshine in a house.

William Makepeace Thackeray

Home is where the heart is.

Pliny

He is happiest, be he king or peasant, who finds peace in his home.

Johann von Goethe

Train up a child in the way he should go: and when he is old, he will not depart from it.

Proverbs 22:6

If we would have a true home, we must guard well our thoughts and actions. 'Tis kindness, gentleness, and love that make the home where peace and blessings dwell.

The experience of living in a warm and loving family relationship is the best preparation children can have against the time when they too will be wives and mothers, husbands and fathers.

Author Unknown

He Gave Up a Fortune to Work for the Lord

Fred C. Crumb serves as a non-salaried chaplain at the Long Beach General Hospital and the El Cerrito Hospital in Long Beach, California.

Fred Crumb is well prepared for his ministry to the lonely and elderly whom he serves, because he knows from experience what true loneliness is like. "My parents separated when I was four," he says. "So as a boy I never knew Christmas, birthday celebrations, or any of the joys of a happy home."

Chaplain Crumb began visiting hospitals when he became a Christian at the age of 12. He fell heir to $250,000.00 as a young man, but he would have had to break his promise to enter full-time Christian service to accept the money under the terms of the will. He is grateful and happy that he honored his decision to serve God.

He married his high school sweetheart and together they graduated from a Bible institute. While still a student he became a full-time chaplain at Cook County Hospital and served there for seven years. His next service as a chaplain was in the county institutions of Maricopa County, Arizona, for four and a half years. During this time he also served as chaplain to the Arizona House of Representatives.

Now more than 600 bedridden people in Long Beach General Hospital and nearby El Cerrito Hospital depend upon Chaplain Crumb for the comfort which normally comes from loved ones and family members. More than 75% of these people are completely forgotten by others. To help them in the battle against loneliness he ministers to mothers and fathers whose children have forgotten them, to neighbors whose friends no longer visit them, to those lonely folks whose loved ones have already passed away and who have been left forgotten and alone.

In an endeavor to fulfill his ministry to those who have outlived their vigor, Chaplain Crumb works a man-sized day. He serves as a non-salaried chaplain to both hospitals and is on call 24 hours a day. Although he reports in at the Long Beach General before 8 A.M. it is often after 6:30 P.M. before he returns home.

Fred Crumb moves like a tornado all day. He practically runs down the long corridors to counsel patients and employees.

It seems a miracle to Fred Crumb that he is working at all. Twenty-seven years ago, a doctor told him that unless he remained absolutely quiet in bed, his heart would stop. But he was sure that God had work for him to do.

A normal week's activity includes preparing for his wheelchair church which meets outside when the weather is warm; meeting with the hospital administrators; rushing to the bedside of those who need him; conducting the Tuesday, Thursday and Friday Bible classes, and directing three Sunday services. Even so, the most important part of his work is with the individuals he helps each day, and he always takes time for each one.

"Our government is spending millions of dollars for research on the subject of geriatrics," says Chaplain Crumb, "But Christians are doing practically nothing for these people. Churches aren't being built to accommodate wheelchairs and these people who were once pillars in the church are largely forgotten by the congregations they helped to build."

Chaplain Crumb's most outstanding experience in a penal institution took place while he was in Arizona. He introduced the Gospel to a prisoner who had killed his wife, two of his children, and attempted suicide. During the ninety days before his execution, the prisoner dramatically witnessed to the power of Christ. And during the condemned man's last night in the death house, Chaplain Crumb and eleven others joined him in singing and praying. At 11:20 P.M. the convicted slayer convinced his former employer of the claims of Jesus Christ.

The singing and the witness of both the triple slayer and his former employer were recorded by Chaplain Crumb. About 450 people heard that testimony at the dead man's memorial service two days later.

Chaplain Crumb sends an urgent plea to all Christians when he says, "Take time to find out the lost members of your church by searching back in the membership files and find out what has happened to those not accounted for. I believe every Christian has a definite responsibility to the senior citizen in his or her own church, but especially to the lost —who may be lost spiritually as well as having lost actual contact with the church."

Since he knows all lonely people aren't in just two hospitals, Chaplain Crumb has developed the "Adopt-A-Grandparent or Pen Pal" program. Through this program, friends outside can help care for the over 2,000 patients who have been placed in local convalescent hospitals and nursing homes. "These elderly men and women find themselves facing a dreary future," he says, "with never a visit or a letter from anyone—no, not even from a pastor!"

Each outside participant of the "Adopt-A-Grandparent" program writes a letter at least once a month to a person assigned to him. This means remembering his birthday and seasonal holidays with a card or gift, and visiting him if possible.

All these ministries have an unusual effect upon the elderly patients. Many have not received a letter for a long time. The worship services, Bible classes and the kindness of Crumb's volunteers have had a definite therapeutic effect upon these lonely folks.

Chaplain Crumb says, "Anyone can serve the Lord by serving this forgotten group of people. It doesn't require a special education or a lot of expense. A visit, a letter, or an inexpensive gift is a witness for Christ when done in His name. Jesus said, 'Inasmuch as ye have done it unto the least of these my brethren, ye have done it unto me.' "

Song

Stay, stay at home, my heart and rest;
Home-keeping hearts are happiest,
For those that wander they know not where
Are full of trouble and full of care;
  To stay at home is best.

Weary and homesick and distressed,
They wander east, they wander west,
And are baffled and beaten and blown about
By the winds of the wilderness of doubt;
  To stay at home is best.

Then stay at home, my heart, and rest;
The bird is safest in its nest,
Over all that flutter their wings and fly
A hawk is hovering in the sky;
  To stay at home is best.

Henry Wadsworth Longfellow

Finding Happiness

"We have a little room in the third story (back), with white curtains trimmed with evergreen, and are as happy as two mortals can be," wrote the poet Lowell.

There is often more happiness in a cottage than in a castle. If it were true that the secret of happiness is riches, then millionaires would be the happiest people on earth, and we are not at all sure that that is true. Do you remember the story of the king who ordered that he be brought the shirt of the happiest man in his kingdom? They found the man—but he didn't have a shirt.

Happiness isn't far off somewhere in the land of tomorrow. It doesn't depend upon a large bank account or a big automobile. We can find it right where we are today by looking for it in simple things, by greeting life as an adventure, by holding thoughts of love and cheer and goodwill.

What happiness there is in good books, a quiet talk, a baby's smile, soft music, clean white sheets, a brisk walk in the fresh air, and the joy of loving and being loved!

If we approach life in the right spirit we shall find happiness every day as we go along.

I Think That God Is Proud

I think that God is proud of those who bear
A sorrow bravely—proud indeed of them
Who walk straight through the dark to find Him there
And kneel in faith to touch His garment's hem.
Oh, proud of them who lift their heads to shake
Away the tears from eyes that have grown dim,
Who tighten quivering lips and turn to take
The only road they know that leads to Him.

How proud He must be of them—He who knows
All sorrow, and how hard grief is to bear!
I think He sees them coming, and He goes
With outstretched arms and hands to meet them there,
And with a look, a touch on hand or head,
Each finds his hurt heart strangely comforted.

Grace Noll Crowell

Morning Prayer

When little things would irk me, and I grow
Impatient with my dear ones, make me know
How in a moment joy can take its flight
And happiness be quenched in endless night.
Keep this thought with me all the livelong day
That I may guard the harsh words I might say
When I would fret and grumble, fiery hot,
At trifles that tomorrow are forgot—
Let me remember, Lord, how it would be
If these, my loved ones, were not here with me.

Author Unknown

Peace
"My peace," the peace of the Lord Most High,
The peace of the Master passing by.
Be this in our home, by night, by day,
Be this our joy if we go or stay.
Margaret E. Sangster

American Heritage

The New Colossus

Not like the brazen giant of Greek fame,
With conquering limbs astride from land to land,
Here at our sea-washed, sunset gates shall stand
A mighty woman with a torch, whose flame
Is the imprisoned lightning, and her name
Mother of Exiles. From her beacon-hand
Glows world-wide welcome; her mild eyes command
The air-bridged harbor that twin cities frame.
"Keep, ancient lands, your storied pomp!" cries she
With silent lips. "Give me your tired, your poor,
Your huddled masses yearning to breathe free,
The wretched refuse of your teeming shore.
Send these, the homeless, tempest-tossed to me,
I lift my lamp beside the golden door!"

Emma Lazarus

On Hay Island, during the Revolutionary War, some hungry and dispirited soldiers dragged themselves and their wounded comrades into an old barn. The tide of battle was against them, and they were discouraged. At that moment General George Washington entered the barn and gave the men the truth about their situation as he said, *"I promise those who will follow me further, no chance of victory, for by my God, I see none; no glory or gain, or laurels returning home, but rather wounds and death, cold and disease and hunger, winters to come such as this, with our bloody trail in the snow, and no end to it till you shovel each other in with those at Valley Forge!"*

As the weary soldiers prepared to bury a dead comrade, General Washington faced them with thoughtful and almost bitter words: *"This liberty will look easy by and by when nobody dies to get it."*

From *Valley Forge* by Maxwell Anderson

America's Mothers

[*Letter to Mrs. Bixby, November 21, 1864*]

I have been shown in the files of the War Department a statement of the Adjutant-General of Massachusetts that you are the mother of five sons who have died gloriously on the field of battle. I feel how weak and fruitless must be any words of mine which should attempt to beguile you from the grief of a loss so overwhelming. But I cannot refrain from tendering to you the consolation that may be found in the thanks of the Republic they died to save. I pray that our heavenly Father may assuage the anguish of your bereavement, and leave you only the cherished memory of the loved and lost, and the solemn pride that must be yours to have laid so costly a sacrifice upon the altar of freedom.

Abraham Lincoln

On the banks of the James River, a husband erected a tombstone in memory of his wife, one of those 100 maidens who had come to Virginia in 1619 to marry the lonely settlers. The stone bore this legend: "She touched the soil of Virginia with her little foot and the wilderness became a home."

Eudora Ramsay Richardson

I am not accustomed to the use of the language of eulogy; I have never studied the art of paying compliments to women; but I must say, that if all that has been said by orators and poets since the creation of the world in praise of women were applied to the women of America, it would not do them justice for their conduct during this war. I will close by saying, God bless the women of America!

Abraham Lincoln

Pioneer Mother

The greatest words could not record
The epic of her years,
Nor tell of hope and hardihood
She shared with pioneers.
She lived a life of stalwart faith,
Expressed in phrase and deed.
Christ walked beside her as she went
To help a friend in need.
Enshrined beyond all tribute words
Of transitory pen,
Her life has been inscribed by love
Within the hearts of men.

Gail Brook Burket

America

It is stories told. It is the Pilgrims dying in their first dreadful winter. It is the Minute Man standing his ground at Concord Bridge, and dying there. It is the army in rags, sick, freezing, starving at Valley Forge. It is the wagons and the men on foot going westward over Cumberland Gap, floating down the great rivers, rolling over the great plains. It is the settler hacking fiercely at the primeval forest on his new, his own lands. It is Thoreau at Walden Pond, Lincoln at Cooper Union, and Lee riding home from Appomattox. It is corruption and disgrace, answered always by men who would not let the flag lie in the dust, who have stood up in every generation to fight for the old ideals and the old rights, at risk of ruin or of life itself.

It is a great multitude of people on pilgrimage, common and ordinary people, charged with the usual human failings, yet filled with such a hope as never caught the imaginations and the hearts of any nation on earth before. The hope of liberty. The hope of justice. The hope of a land in which a man can stand straight, without fear, without rancor.

The land and the people and the flag—the land a continent, the people of every race, the flag a symbol of what humanity may aspire to when the wars are over and the barriers are down; to these each generation must be dedicated and consecrated anew, to defend with life itself, if need be, but, above all, in friendliness, in hope, in courage, to live for.

Anonymous

Chant of Loyalty

Firm as the furnace heat
Rivets the bars of steel,
Thus to thy destiny,
  Flag, are we plighted;
One are the hearts that beat,
One is the throb we feel,
One in our loyalty,
  Stand we united.

Many a folk have brought
Sinew and brawn to thee;
Many an ancient wrong
  Well hast thou righted;
Here in the land we sought,
Stanchly, from sea to sea,
Here, where our hearts belong,
  Stand we united.

Ask us to pay the price,
All that we have to give,
Nothing shall be denied,
  All be requited;
Ready for sacrifice,
Ready for thee to live,
Over the country wide
  Stand we united.

One under palm and pine,
One in the prairie sun,
One on the rock-bound shore,
  Liberty-sighted;
All that we have is thine,
Thine, who hast made us one,
True to thee evermore,
  Stand we united.

Elias Lieberman

Barbara Frietchie

Up from the meadows rich with corn.
Clear in the cool September morn,

The clustered spires of Frederick stand
Green-walled by the hills of Maryland.

Round about them orchards sweep,
Apple and peach-tree fruited deep,

Fair as a garden of the Lord
To the eyes of the famished rebel horde,

On that pleasant morn of the early fall
When Lee marched over the mountain wall;

Over the mountains winding down,
Horse and foot, into Frederick town.

Forty flags with their silver stars,
Forty flags with their crimson bars,

Flapped in the morning wind: the sun
Of noon looked down, and saw not one.

Up rose old Barbara Frietchie then,
Bowed with her fourscore years and ten;

Bravest of all in Frederick town,
She took up the flag the men hauled down;

In her attic window the staff she set,
To show that one heart was loyal yet.

Up the street came the rebel tread,
Stonewall Jackson riding ahead.

Under his slouched hat left and right
He glanced; the old flag met his sight.

"Halt!"—the dust-brown ranks stood fast.
"Fire!"—out blazed the rifle blast.

It shivered the window, pane and sash;
It rent the banner with seam and gash.

Quick, as it fell, from the broken staff
Dame Barbara snatched the silken scarf.

She leaned far out on the window-sill,
And shook it forth with a royal will.

"Shoot, if you must, this old grey head,
But spare your country's flag," she said.

A shade of sadness, a blush of shame,
Over the face of the leader came;

The nobler nature within him stirred
To life at that woman's deed and word;

"Who touches a hair of yon grey head
Dies like a dog! March on!" he said.

All day long through Frederick street
Sounded the tread of marching feet:

All day long that free flag tost
Over the heads of the rebel host.

Ever its torn folds rose and fell
On the loyal winds that loved it well;

And through the hill-gaps sunset light
Shone over it with a warm good-night.

Barbara Frietchie's work is o'er,
And the rebel rides on his raids no more.

Honor to her! and let a tear
Fall, for her sake, on Stonewall's bier.

Over Barbara Frietchie's grave,
Flag of freedom and union, wave!

Peace, and order, and beauty draw
Round thy symbol of light and law;

And ever the stars above look down
On thy stars below in Frederick town!

John Greenleaf Whittier

The Home and the Republic

I went to Washington the other day, and as I stood on Capitol Hill my heart beat quickly as I looked at the towering marble of my Country's Capitol, and the mist gathered in my eyes as I thought of its tremendous significance, the armies, and the Treasury, and the Courts, and Congress and the President, and all that was gathered there. And I felt that the sun in all its course could not look down upon a better sight than that majestic home of the Republic that had taught the world its best lessons in liberty.

Two days afterwards I went to visit a friend in the country, a modest man, with a quiet country home. It was just a simple, unpretentious house, set about with great trees, encircled in meadow and fields rich with the promise of harvest. The fragrance of pink and hollyhock in the front yard was mingled with the aroma of the orchard and of the garden, and resonant with the cluck of poultry and the hum of bees. Inside was quiet, cleanliness, thrift and comfort. Outside there stood my friend—master of his land and master of himself. There was his old father, an aged, trembling man, happy in the heart and home of his son. And as they started to their home the hands of the old man went down on the young man's shoulders, laying there the unspeakable blessing of an honored and grateful father, and ennobling it with the knighthood of the fifth commandment.

And I saw the night come down on that home, falling gently as from the wings of an unseen dove, and the old man, while a startled bird called from the forest, and the trees shrilled with the cricket's cry, and the stars were swarming in the sky, got the family around him, and taking the old Bible from the table, called them to their knees, while he closed the record of that simple day by calling down God's blessing on that family and that home. And while I gazed, the vision of the marble Capitol faded. Forgotten were its treasures and its majesty, and I said: "O surely, here in the hearts of the people, at least are lodged the strength and responsibilities of this government, the hope and promise of this Republic."

Henry W. Grady

The Promised Land

It was my habit to go very slowly up the low, broad steps to the palace entrance, pleasing my eyes with the majestic lines of the building, and lingering to read again the carved inscriptions: *Public Library—Built by the People—Free to All.*

Did I not say it was my palace? Mine, because I was a citizen; mine, though I was born an alien; mine, though I lived on Dover Street. My palace—*mine!*

I loved to lean against a pillar in the entrance hall, watching the people go in and out. Groups of children hushed their chatter at the entrance, and skipped, whispering and giggling in their fists, up the grand stairway, patting the great stone lions at the top, with an eye on the aged policemen down below. Spectacled scholars came slowly down the stairs, loaded with books, heedless of the lofty arches that echoed their steps. Visitors from out of town lingered long in the entrance hall, studying the inscriptions and symbols on the marble floor. And I loved to stand in the midst of all this, and remind myself that I was there, that I had a right to be there, that I was at home there. All these eager children, all these fine-browed women, all these scholars going home to write learned books—I and they had this glorious thing in common, this noble treasure house of learning. It was wonderful to say, *This is mine;* it was thrilling to say, *This is ours.*

Sitting on the steps of the Boston Public Library, where the treasures of the whole of human thought had been opened to me, I wrote, "This is my latest home, and it invites me to a glad new life. The endless ages have indeed throbbed through my blood, but a new rhythm dances in my veins. My spirit is not tied to the monumental past, any more than my feet were bound to my grandfather's house below the hill. The past was only my cradle, and now it cannot hold me, because I am grown too big; just as the little house in Polotzk, once my home, has now become a toy of memory, as I move about at will in the wide spaces of this splendid palace, whose shadow covers acres. No! It is not I that belong to the past, but the past that belongs to me. America is the youngest of the nations, and inherits all that went before in history. And I am the youngest of America's children, and into my hands is given all her priceless heritage, to the last white star espied through the telescope, to the last great thought of the philosopher. Mine is the whole majestic past, and mine the shining future."

Here is where I liked to remind myself of Polotzk, the better to bring out the wonder of my life. That I who was born in the prison of the Pale should roam at will in the land of freedom was a marvel that it did me good to realize. That I who was brought up to my teens almost without a book should be set down in the midst of all the books that ever were written was a miracle as great as any on record. That an outcast should become a privileged citizen, that a beggar should dwell in a palace—this was a romance more thrilling than poet ever sung. Surely I was rocked in an enchanted cradle. . . .

Marie Antin

A Mighty Bulwark

When that indomitable soldier, acclaimed by many to be "the greatest military genius ever born on this side of the Atlantic, Stonewall Jackson lay dead on the battlefield at Chancellorsville, one of his devoted officers, bending low over the lifeless corpse, touched the cold hand and said:

"If you meet with Caesar tonight, tell him we still make war."

We, who are members of that goodly company which for nineteen centuries has fought in every land under the banner of the gentle Christ, proclaim to the world that we "still make war" against all the forces that would undermine the sanctity of the home and the integrity of the family life. May we not ask our fellow citizens of every faith to join with us in fighting for the permanence of the home, the sacredness of conjugal love, and the sanctity of the family fireside around which are enshrined the noblest traditions of our American life? In thus struggling for the preservation of the institutions of the home and the family in all the beauty of their unity and integrity, we are struggling for the maintenance of the mightiest bulwark for the preservation of the America we love so much.

John A. O'Brien

Mine Eyes Have Seen the Glory

Mine eyes have seen the glory of the coming of the Lord:
He is trampling out the vintage where the grapes of wrath are stored;
He hath loosed the fateful lightning of his terrible swift sword:
His truth is marching on.

I have seen him in the watch-fires of a hundred circling camps,
They have builded him an altar in the evening dews and damps;
I can read his righteous sentence by the dim and flaring lamps:
His day is marching on.

He has sounded forth the trumpet that shall never call retreat;
He is sifting out the hearts of men before His judgment seat.
Oh, be swift, my soul, to answer Him! be jubilant, my feet!
Our God is marching on.

In the beauty of the lilies Christ was born across the sea;
With a glory in His bosom that transfigures you and me;
As He died to make men holy, let us die to make men free,
While God is marching on.

Julia Ward Howe

Golden Thoughts

For what avail the plough or sail, Or land or life, if freedom fail?

Ralph Waldo Emerson

Let us, at all times remember that all American citizens are brothers of a common country, and should dwell together in the bonds of fraternal feeling.

Abraham Lincoln

The greatest glory of a freeborn people is to transmit that freedom to their children.

Then join hand in hand, brave Americans all; By uniting we stand, by dividing we fall.

John Dickinson

Let us raise a standard to which the wise and honest can repair; the rest is in the hands of God.

George Washington

I say the real and permanent grandeur of these United States must be their religion.

Walt Whitman

The people are the only sure reliance for the preservation of our liberty.

Thomas Jefferson

I believe in God, and I trust myself in His hands.

This Land and Flag

What is the love of country for which our flag stands? Maybe it begins with love of the land itself. It is the fog rolling in with the tide at Eastport, or through the Golden Gate and among the towers of San Francisco. It is the sun coming up behind the White Mountains, over the Green, throwing a shining glory on Lake Champlain and above the Adirondacks. It is the storied Mississippi rolling swift and muddy past St. Louis, rolling past Cairo, pouring down past the levees of New Orleans. It is lazy noontide in the pines of Carolina, it is a sea of wheat rippling in western Kansas, it is the San Francisco peaks far north across the glowing nakedness of Arizona, it is the Grand Canyon, and a little stream coming down out of a New England ridge, in which are trout.

It is men at work. It is the storm-tossed fishermen coming into Gloucester and Provincetown and Astoria. It is the farmer riding his great machine in the dust of harvest, the dairyman going to the barn before sunrise, the lineman mending the broken wire, the miner drilling for the blast. It is the servants of fire in the murky splendor of Pittsburgh, between the Allegheny and the Monongahela, the trucks rumbling through the night, the locomotive engineer bringing the train in on time, the pilot in the clouds, the riveter running along the beam a hundred feet in air. It is the clerk in the office, the housewife doing the dishes and sending the children off to school. It is the teacher, doctor, and parson tending and helping body and soul for small reward.

It is small things remembered: The little corners of the land, the houses, the people that each one loves. We love our country because there was a little tree on a hill, and grass thereon, and a sweet valley below; because the hurdy-gurdy man came along on a sunny morning in a city street; because a beach or a farm or a lane or a house that might not seem much to others was once, for each of us, made magic. It is voices that are remembered only, no longer heard. It is parents, friends, the lazy chat of street and store and office, and the ease of mind that makes life tranquil. It is summer and winter, rain and sun and storm. These are flesh of our flesh, bone of our bone, blood of our blood, a lasting part of what we are, each of us and all of us together.

Freedom from Fear

A hundred and sixty odd years ago, we, as a nation, asserted that all men were created equal, that all men were entitled to life, liberty and the pursuit of happiness. Those were large assertions, but we have tried to live up to them. We have not always succeeded, we have often failed. But our will and desire as a nation has been to live up to them.

Now, in concert with other free nations, we say that those children you see and other children like them all over the world shall grow to manhood and womanhood free from fear.

We say they shall have a chance, and an equal chance, to grow and develop and lead the lives they choose to lead, not lives mapped out for them by a master. And we say that freedom for ourselves involves freedom for others—that it is a universal right, neither lightly given by Providence nor to be maintained by words alone, but by acts and deeds and living.

We who are alive today did not make our free institutions. We got them from the men of the past and we hold them in trust for the future. Should we put ease and selfishness above them, that trust will fail and we shall lose all, not a portion or a degree of liberty, but all that has been built for us and all that we hope to build.

Real peace will not be won with one victory. It can be won only by long determination, firm resolve and a wish to share and work with other men, no matter what their race or creed or condition. And yet, we do have the choice. We can have freedom from fear.

Stephen Vincent Benet

Col. Ellsworth's Last Letter to His Parents

"Washington, May 23, 1867.

"My Dear Father and Mother,—The regiment is ordered to move across the river tonight. We have no means of knowing what reception we are to meet with. I am inclined to the opinion that our entrance to the city of Alexandria will be hotly contested, as I am informed a large force has arrived there to-day. Should this happen, my dear parents, it may be my lot to be injured in some manner. Whatever may happen, cherish the consolation that I was engaged in the performance of a sacred duty; and to-night, thinking over the probabilities of tomorrow, and the occurences of the past, I am perfectly content to accept whatever my fortune may be, confident that He who noteth even the fall of a sparrow, will have some purpose even in the fate of one like me. My darling and ever loved parents, good bye. God bless, protect and care for you.

"Elmer"

So Long!

This father speaks here for all fathers whose sons go off to war.

There was no band, no flags, no ceremonial. It wasn't even dramatic. A car honked outside and he said: "Well, I guess that's for me." He picked up his little bag, and his mother said: "You haven't forgotten your gloves?"

He kissed his mother and held out his hand to me. "Well, so long," he said. I took his hand but all I could say was "Good luck."

The door slammed and that was that—another boy gone to war.

I had advised waiting for the draft—waiting at least until he was required to register. I had pointed out that he was not yet of age. He had smiled at that, and assured me that his mind was made up. He wanted peace, he said. Without peace, what good was living?

There was finality in the way he said this—a finality at once grim and gentle. I said no more about waiting.

After the door closed behind him I went upstairs. I went to what had been his room. It was in worse chaos than usual. His bureau was littered—an incredible collection of things, letters, keys, invitations to parties he would not attend.

Clothing was scattered about—a tennis racket, his precious collection of phonograph records, his trumpet, gleaming in its case.

I went then to my room. On the wall was a picture of a little boy, his toothless grin framed in tawny curls—the same boy who had just taken my hand and said: "Well, so long."

Not much time, I thought, between the making of that picture and the slamming of the front door. Not much more than a decade.

Suddenly, a queer thing happened. Objects came alive—whispered to me. The house was full of soft voices. They led me up to the attic—to a box of toy soldiers, a broken music rack, a football helmet, a home-made guitar, school books, class pictures, a stamp album, a penny bank with the lid pried off . . . ancient history, long hidden under dust.

The voices led me on to a filing case and a folder stuffed with papers—report cards, letters—among them the wail of an exasperated teacher: "Though he looks like an angel . . ."—telegrams, passports, a baptismal certificate, a ribbon won in a track meet, faded photographs—one taken on the memorable first day of long pants—a bit of golden hair.

I sat down and thought how time had flown. Why, it was only yesterday when I had held him in my arms! That, somehow, made me remember all the scoldings I had given him, the preachments, the exhortation to a virtue and wisdom I did not myself possess. . . .

I thought, too, of that last inarticulate "good luck," that last perfunctory handclasp; and I wished that I had somehow been able to tell him how much I really loved him. Had he perhaps penetrated my brusque reserve? Had he perhaps guessed what was in my heart?

And then I thought: what fools we are with our children—always plotting what we shall make of them, always planning for a future that never comes, always intent on what they may be, never accepting what they are.

Well, curly-head—you're a man now, bearing your bright new shield and spear. I hated to see you go out of my house and close the door behind you; but I think I would not have halted you if I could. I salute you, sir. I cannot pretend that I am not sad; but I am proud, too. So long.

Howard Vincent O'Brien

Peace Hymn of the Republic

O Lord, our God, Thy mighty hand
  Hath made our country free;
From all her broad and happy land
  May praise arise to Thee.
Fulfil the promise of her youth,
  Her liberty defend;
By law and order, love and truth,
  America befriend!

The strength of every state increase
  In Union's golden chain;
Her thousand cities fill with peace,
  Her million fields with grain.
The virtues of her mingled blood
  In one new people blend;
By unity and brotherhood
  America befriend!

Through all the waiting land proclaim
  Thy gospel of good-will;
And may the music of Thy name
  In every bosom thrill.
O'er hill and vale, from sea to sea,
  Thy holy reign extend;
By faith and hope and charity,
  America befriend!

Henry van Dyke

So Long as There Are Homes

So long as there are homes to which men turn
At the close of day,
So long as there are homes where children are—
Where women stay,
If love and loyalty and faith be found
Across these sills,
A stricken nation can recover from
Its gravest ills.

So long as there are homes where fires burn
And there is bread,
So long as there are homes where lamps are lit
And prayers are said;
Although a people falters through the dark
And nations grope,
With God himself back of these little homes
We still can hope.

Grace Noll Crowell

Golden Nuggets

I know of no safe depository of the ultimate powers of society but the people themselves; and if we think them not enlightened enough to exercise their control with a wholesome discretion, the remedy is not to take it from them, but to inform their discretion by education.

Thomas Jefferson

We wish that this column, rising towards heaven among the pointed spires of so many temples dedicated to God, may contribute also to produce in all minds a pious feeling of dependence and gratitude. We wish, finally, that the last object to the sight of him who leaves his native shore, and the first to gladden his who revisits it, may be something which shall remind him of the liberty and glory of his country. Let it rise! Let it rise, till it meet the sun in its coming; let the earliest light of the morning gild it, and parting day linger and play on its summit!

Daniel Webster

The Man without a Country

I suppose that very few casual readers of the *New York Herald* of August 13, 1863, noticed, in an obscure corner, among the "Deaths," the announcement,

"NOLAN. Died on board *U.S.S. Corvette Levant,* Lat. 2° 11′ S., Long. 131° W., on the 11th of May, PHILIP NOLAN."

There are hundreds of readers who would have paused at that announcement, if the officer of the *Levant* who reported it had chosen to make it thus: "Died, May 11, 'The Man without a Country.' " For it was as "The Man without a Country" that poor Philip Nolan had generally been known by the officers who had him in charge during some fifty years.

And now that the poor creature is dead, it seems to me worth while to tell a little of his story, by way of showing young Americans of today what it is to be a "Man without a Country."

Philip Nolan was as fine a young officer as there was in the "Legion of the West."

When Aaron Burr made his first dashing expedition to New Orleans in 1805, he met young Nolan at Fort Massac. Burr marked him, took him on a voyage in his flatboat, and fascinated him. For the next year barracks life was very tame to poor Nolan.

Then one day Burr came down the river once again. It was rumored that he had an army behind him and an empire before him. Within an hour of his arrival at the Fort, Burr sent for Nolan; by the end of the evening, Nolan was enlisted heart and soul. When the grand catastrophe came, Nolan's insignificant name appeared on the House of Virginia's list of courts-martial. There was evidence that he was sick of the service and would have been willing to obey any order signed, "By command of His Exec. A. Burr." When Judge Colonel Morgan gave Nolan a chance to vindicate himself with an oath of loyalty, Nolan cried out in a fit of frenzy, "Damn the United States! I wish I may never hear of the United States again!"

Old Morgan called the court into his private room, and returned in fifteen minutes, with a face like a sheet, to say, "Prisoner, hear the sentence of the court! The court decides, subject to the approval of the President, that you never hear the name of the United States again."

Philip Nolan served his sentence and the next fifty-five years were spent on shipboard. And now it seems the dear old fellow is dead. He has found a home at last, and a country.

Since writing this, and considering whether or not I would print it as a warning to the young Nolans of today of what it means to throw away one's country, I have received from Danforth, who is on board the *Levant,* a letter which gives an account of Nolan's last hours. It removes all my doubts about writing this story. Here is the letter:

"Dear Fred,—I try to find heart and life to tell you that it is all over with dear old Nolan. I have been with him on this voyage more than I ever was; and I can understand wholly now the way in which you used to speak of the dear old fellow. I could see that he was not strong, but I had no idea the end was so near. The doctor had been watching him —and he said he should like to see me.

"Well, I went in, and there, to be sure, the poor fellow lay in his berth, smiling pleasantly as he gave me his hand, but looking very frail. I could not help a glance round. The Stars and Stripes were triced up above and around a picture of Washington, and he had painted a majestic eagle, with lightnings blazing from his beak, and his foot just clasping the whole globe, which his wings overshadowed. The dear old boy saw my glance, and said with a sad smile, 'Here, you see, I have a country!" And then he pointed to the foot of his bed, where I had not seen before a great map of the United States, as he had drawn it from memory, and which he had there to look upon as he lay. Quaint, queer old names were on it in large letters: 'Indiana Territory,' 'Mississippi Territory,' and 'Louisiana Territory,' as I suppose our fathers learned such things; but the old fellow had patched in Texas, too; he had carried his Western boundary all the way to the Pacific.

"'Oh, Danforth,' he said, 'I know I am dying. I cannot get home. Surely you will tell me something now? Stop! stop! Do not speak till I say what I am sure you know, that there is not in this ship, that there is not in America—God bless her!—a more loyal man than I. There cannot be a man who loves the old flag as I do, or prays for it as I do, or hopes for it as I do. There are thirty-four stars in it now, Danforth. I thank God for that, though I do not know what their names are. There has never been one taken away; I thank God for that. I know by that, that there has never been any successful Burr. Oh, Danforth, Danforth,' he sighed out, 'how like a wretched night's dream a boy's idea of personal fame or of separate sovereignty seems, when one looks back on it after such a life as mine! But tell me everything, Danforth, before I die!'

"Ingham, I swear to you that I felt like a monster that I had not told him everything before. Danger or no danger, who was I, that I should have been acting the tyrant all this time over this dear, sainted old man, who had years ago expiated, in his whole manhood's life, the madness of a boy's treason? 'Mr. Nolan,' said I, 'I will tell you everything.'

"Oh, the blessed smile that crept over his white face! and he pressed my hand, and said, 'God bless you! Tell me their names,' he said, and he pointed to the stars on the flag. 'The last I know is Ohio. My father lived in Kentucky. But I have guessed Michigan and Indiana and Mississippi,—that was where Fort Adams is; they make twenty. But where are your other fourteen?

"I told him the names in as good order as I could, and he bade me take down his beautiful map, and draw them in as best I could. He was wild with delight about Texas, told me how his cousin died there. Then he was delighted as he saw California and Oregon; that he said he had suspected partly, because he had never been permitted to land on that shore. Then he settled down more quietly and very happily, to hear me tell in an hour the history of fifty years. I told him of the English war. I told him about Fulton and the steamboat beginning. I told him about old Scott and Jackson; told him all I could think of about the Mississippi and New Orleans and Texas and his own old Kentucky.

"I tell you, Ingham, it was a hard thing to condense the history of half a century into that talk with a sick man. And I do not now know what I told him,—of emigration, and the means of it; of steamboats and railroads and telegraphs; of inventions and books and literature; of the colleges and West Point and the Naval School.

"I remember he asked, all of a sudden, who was President now; and when I told him, he asked if Old Abe was General Benjamin Lincoln's son. I said No, that Old Abe was a Kentuckian like himself, but I could not tell him of what family; he had worked up from the ranks. 'Good for him!' cried Nolan; 'I am glad of that. I have thought our danger was in keeping up those regular successions in the first families.' Then I got talking about my visit to Washington. I told him about the Smithsonian and the Exploring Expedition; I told him about the Capitol and the statues for the pediment and Crawford's Liberty and Greenough's Washington. Ingham, I told him everything I could think of that would show the grandeur of his country.

"And he drank it in, and enjoyed it as I cannot tell you.

"Then he asked me to bring the Presbyterian *Book of Public Prayer*, which lay there, and said with a smile that it would open at the right place,—and so it did. There was his double red mark down the page; and I knelt down and read, and he repeated with me: 'For ourselves and our country, O gracious God, we thank Thee that notwithstanding our manifold transgressions of Thy holy laws, Thou hast continued to us Thy marvelous kindness,'—and so to the end of that Thanksgiving. Then he turned to the end of the same book, and I read the words more familiar to me: 'Most heartily we beseech Thee with Thy favor to behold and bless Thy servant, the President of the United States, and all others in authority,'—and the rest of the Episcopal Collect. 'Danforth,' said he, 'I have repeated those prayers night and morning, it is now fifty-five years.' Then he said he would go to sleep, 'Look in my Bible, Danforth, when I am gone.' And I went away.

"But I had no thought it was the end. I thought he was tired and would sleep. I knew he was happy, and I wanted him to be alone.

"But in an hour, when the doctor went in gently, he found Nolan had breathed his life away with a smile. He had something pressed close to his lips. It was his father's badge of the Order of the Cincinnati.

"We looked in his Bible, and there was a slip of paper at the place where he had marked the text,

" 'They desire a country, even a heavenly: wherefore God is not ashamed to be called their God: for he hath prepared for them a city.'

"On this slip of paper he had written, Bury me in the sea; it has been my home, and I love it. But will not some one set up a stone for my memory at Fort Adams or at Orleans, that my disgrace may not be more than I ought to bear? Say on it,

In Memory of
PHILIP NOLAN,
Lieutenant in the Army of the United States.

He loved his country as no other man has loved her;
but no man deserved less at her hands.' "

Edward Everett Hale

Thanksgiving

What To Be Thankful For

Oh, Lord, I thank You for the privilege and gift of living in a world filled with beauty and excitement and variety.

I thank You for the gift of loving and being loved, for the friendliness and understanding and beauty of the animals on the farm and in the forest and marshes, for the green of the trees, the sound of a waterfall, the darting beauty of the trout in the brook.

I thank You for the delights of music and children, of other men's thoughts and conversations and their books to read by the fireside or in bed with the rain falling on the roof or the snow blowing past outside the window.

I thank You for the beauties of the four seasons and of the churches and the houses built by fellow men that stand throughout the centuries as monuments to man's aspirations and sense of beauty.

I thank You for the powers of mind which find in the universe an endless and inexhaustible source of interest and fascination, for the understanding of so many elements which make life precious.

I thank You for all the senses You have bestowed upon me and for the delights which they bring me. I thank You for my body itself which is so wonderful and delightful a mechanism.

I thank You for the smile on the face of a woman, for the touch of a friend's hand, for the laughter of a child, the wagging tail of a dog and the touch of his cold nose against my face.

I thank You for all these things and many more, and above all I thank You for people with all their goodness and understanding which so far outweigh their vices, their envy, their deceits.

Thank You, God, for life itself, without which the universe would have no meaning.

Louis Bromfield

We must not hope to be mowers,
And to gather the ripe gold ears,
Unless we have first been sowers
And watered the furrows with tears.

It is not just as we take it,
This mystical world of ours,
Life's field will yield as we make it
A harvest of thorns or of flowers.

Johann W. von Goethe

We Give Thee Thanks

For love of friends who share with us the treasures
  That life to them has bountifully bestowed;
For love of home; for parents, warmth and shelter;
  for cheering words of neighbors as they share our load;
For nights with stars; for healing rays of sunshine;
  For birds and flow'rs; for trees; for hills to climb—
O Lord, for all these precious gifts of mercy
  We give Thee thanks . . . at this Thanksgivingtime.

For ears that thrill to hear the heav'nly music
  That fills our lives with beauty, rich and deep;
For eyes to see the grandeur of creation;
  For times of study . . . times of blessed sleep;
For blessed knowledge of our soul's salvation;
  For quiet times with Thee . . . when bells do chime—
O Lord, for all these precious gifts of mercy
  We give Thee thanks . . . at this Thanksgivingtime.

But most of all, we give Thee thanks, dear Father,
  For Jesus our Redeemer, Helper, Friend,
Who sticketh closer than the dearest brother,
  Who saves and keeps us to the very end;
For blessed hope of Christ the Lord's returning
  As written in Thy Holy Word sublime—
O Lord, for all these precious gifts of mercy
  We give Thee thanks . . . at this Thanksgivingtime.

Charlotte M. Kruger

Rich Though Poor

Some years ago, during the depression, a government agent traveled through the Tennessee Mountains making small allotments to impoverished farmers for seed, stock or needed improvements. He found one woman who lived alone, scratching out a bare living on two acres of barren ground. "If the government should allot you $200, what would you do with it?" he asked her.

The woman thought a moment. Her cabin had no floor, its windows were covered with tar paper, light came through the broken walls. Finally, she looked up. "Reckon I'd give it to the poor," she said.

F. Emerson Andrews

Why Bobby Changed His Mind

Day after tomorrow's *Thanksgiving Day,* and Teacher said she wanted us to tell her tomorrow what we had to be thankful for. What do *I* have to be thankful for, I should like to know! *Nothing!* I wanted to stay at the farm all winter and have fun snowshoeing and sledding on the hills and I had to come home and go to *school*!"

The way Bobby said "school" would have made the poor old school squirm if it had been anywhere near and had had ears to hear!

"And I want a bicycle," continued Bobby, "but Mother says she can't afford it. And I have to go to bed at eight o'clock (Bobby was in bed at this moment!) and there are boys playing ball out there right now—I can hear them. I've got a lot to be thankful for! I should say not! I'll just tell Teacher so tomorrow!"

And Bobby did. He recited all his woes to her, and Miss Langdon looked very grave—because, of course, she was so sorry for him, Bobby thought.

When school was over, Miss Langdon said, "I want to take you somewhere, Bobby; will you come?"

Bobby's face brightened. She must be going to take him to the bicycle shop to show him how cheaply he could get a bicycle, so that he could tell Mother. Bobby knew it!

"We'll call at your house on the way, Bobby," she said, "and tell Mother, so that she will not be anxious."

When they left Bobby's home, they took their way to the outskirts of the village. "She isn't going to the bicycle shop after all to show me how cheaply I can get a bicycle," thought Bobby mournfully. Miss Langdon stopped a moment at her own house and brought out a big basket. She did not offer to tell what was in it, and Bobby's curiosity grew as he helped her carry it down the street.

They went on until they came to the poorest house Bobby had ever seen in his life. Miss Langdon knocked on the door, and a squeaky little voice said, "Come in!" When they passed through the door, Bobby wondered where the voice had come from. He saw no one. The only furniture in the room was an unpainted table without a cloth, one wooden chair, a kitchen stove propped up with bricks where one leg was missing, and what looked like a big box in a far corner. Miss Langdon crossed to the box and bent over it. She turned and called to Bobby. When he reached the box, he saw that in it was a boy about his own age. But what a different boy!

"Do you want to see my kitten?" he asked Bobby. Bobby managed to say, "Yes," and the boy drew from under the blanket a soft little bunch of gray fur. "Isn't it lovely?" he asked. "It doesn't belong to me, because we can't afford to feed a kitten. It needs milk, and Mother has all she can do to buy milk for me. But Teddy Kane lends it to me for two hours every day, to keep me company while Mother's out. Don't you think I'm a lucky boy? Mother hadn't been going out until two days ago. She couldn't get work. That is why we haven't a fire in the stove. Mother says she'll get around to buying wood very soon, but she had to buy food first. But I'm not cold now"—he said it eagerly as if to make sure they would not think that he was grumbling—"this blanket's *great*! Don't you want to hold my kitten?" the boy added.

Bobby hardly heard him. "Why—why do you have a bed like this?" he managed to ask.

"Oh, that's another blessing," the boy answered. "Mother says the sides keep me warm. There'd be drafts if it were only a cot bed. Mother had to sell the big bed, and Teddy Kane's daddy made this for me. If Mother hadn't had to sell the big bed, I'd have had to sleep in the drafts."

Bobby looked up at Miss Langdon. Here was something he couldn't understand at all. The idea of being thankful for a box instead of a bed!

"I've brought something for dinner for you and your mother," she said. And now Bobby learned what Teacher had in the basket they had carried. She first took out a pie. "It's a meat pie, Lennie," she said. "Mother had better warm it. There's lots of gravy." Next she took out two loaves of bread and a pound of butter, and then some pears and apples. "And here's some coffee and sugar and canned milk for Mother. Now, Lennie, we're ready for Thanksgiving Day, aren't we? And there's a whole cord of wood, cut and split, ready for the stove, coming this minute. I see it out there now! Where shall I tell them to put it, Lennie?"

"At the back of the house, lady. Oh, lady! Won't Mother be glad! And would they bring some in and put it by the stove?"

"I'll do that," cried Bobby, glad to find a way to help. He ran out and told the man where to put the wood, and asked if he might have an armful to carry in. When he went in with it, he found that there was a woman with Teacher and Lennie. He realized at once that she was Lennie's mother. The sick boy was excitedly giving her a list of the wonderful things on the table.

Teacher was very quiet on the way home. Bobby finally spoke. "Can't he get out of bed at all, Teacher?"

"No, Bobby; his back and legs are crippled."

"O-oh!" said Bobby. Presently he ventured again. "Teacher, I'm *sorry* I said I hadn't anything to be thankful for. Why, I have *heaps*! I've too many things to name them! Why, there's my being able to walk —and my home—and a turkey tomorrow—and my warm bed, and—so *many* things. Lennie said he couldn't read 'cause he'd never been able to go to school—so I've got to be thankful I can go, and I used to think it was horrid! Teacher, if you ask us next year, I'll make a big list to give you, 'cause there *is* a big list. I think Lennie is the thankfullest boy I know, 'cause he has hardly anything, has he?"

"Bobby," said Teacher, "I hoped you would understand. Everybody living has *something* to be thankful for! And the most wonderful thing is that God loves us so—loves us so much that 'he gave his only begotten Son, that whosoever believeth in him should not perish, but have everlasting life.' And even the very poorest person can have this!"

Alice M. Ardagh

Thanksgiving . . . 1950

Hard, hard it is, this anxious autumn,
To lift the heavy mind from its dark forebodings;
To sit at the bright feast, and with ruddy cheer
Give thanks for the harvest of a troubled year.
The clouds move and shift, withdraw to new positions on the hills;
The sky above us is a thinning haze—a patch of blue appears—
We yearn toward the blue sky as toward the healing of all our ills;
But the storm has not gone over; the clouds come back;
The blue sky turns black;
And the muttering thunder suddenly crashes close, and once again
Flashes of lightning startle the rattling windowpane;
Then once more pours and splashes down the cold, discouraging rain.
Ah, but is it right to feast in a time so solemn?
Should we not, rather, fast—and give the day to prayer?
Prayer, yes; but fasting, no.
Soldier and citizen alike, we are a marching column,
And how long the march may be, and over what terrain
We do not know;
Nor how much of hardship, and hunger, how much of pain
We may be called upon to endure. And fortitude
Takes muscle; and needs food.
Never more dear than in a thoughtful hour like this
Are the faces about the table: each stands out
More sharply than before, and is looked at with a longer glance.
And smiles are deep, from behind the eyes, and somewhat quizzical,
Lest they go too far in tenderness.
God bless the harvest of this haggard year;
Pity our hearts, that did so long for Peace;
Deal with us kindly: there are many here
Who love their fellow man (and may their tribe increase).
But cunning and guile persist; ferocity empowers
The lifted arm of the aggressor: the times are bad.
Let us give thanks for the courage that was always ours;
And pray for the wisdom which we never had.
This is nothing new—that we should be attacked
While we are napping: is it not always so?—
And, dazed and unprepared, start up to act,
Rubbing our eyes, not knowing where to go?
From the apprehensive present, from a future packed
With unknown dangers, monstrous, terrible and new—
Let us turn for comfort to this simple fact:
We have been in trouble before . . . and we came through.

Edna St. Vincent Millay

The Tread of Footsteps

The pleasant memory of a grateful mother who held fast to the belief that "God will light the dark places" forever weaves a pattern in one's life. Her fortitude of soul and valor of heart held to faith in time of trouble.

All through the years, our vegetable garden was sheer delight, and my mother's gratitude for the harvest was unbounded. "The earth nourished our forefathers, it will nourish us and those who come after us. We have security in the earth," she said proudly. Her faith overshadowed our doubt.

There was something hopeful about our adventures. We struggled with floods, drouth, and illness, but we always came out all right. The garden flourished from spring until winter, then faith soared high for the next planting season.

In the dewy cool of a spring morning, plowing the loamy soil was always new and exciting. It was something we inherited with the land itself. I recall fondly, the horse moving rhythmically along the furrows.

When the fields were golden with fruit and grain in autumn, the gratitude of my prudent mother was irrepressible. She invariably affirmed the same belief, "This is the best year of all."

In the faded ash of evening, we sat in the old-fashioned open hall and heard the story of the Pilgrim Fathers landing at Plymouth, and the history of pioneers who carved away the wilderness and helped to settle this free country.

If our Thanksgiving dinner was not elegant and elaborate, my far-seeing mother said discreetly, "We should be thankful. The Pilgrims had to search for wild game for their dinner. They were thankful."

Unshaken faith and unbounded gratitude are comforting traditions to carry through life. Time's fast-moving shuttle does not erase the heritage passed on from parent to child. The tread of such footsteps still echoes through the corridors of time.

Gertie Fry

Autumn

The morns are meeker than they were,
The nuts are getting brown;
The berry's cheek is plumper,
The rose is out of town.
The maple wears a gayer scarf,
The field a scarlet gown.
Lest I should be old-fashioned,
I'll put a trinket on.

Emily Dickinson

"God Has Been Good to Me"

For 25 years I watched him fight cancer of the face. First, just a small speck that began to grow larger; then, year after year, I watched him go to the hospital and have a bit more cut out each time. As the years went by, his face was hardly a face at all as more and more was cut away. But always when he returned, with what was left of that face, he tried to smile and never once uttered a complaint or seemed to be downhearted.

He was a skilled mechanic and finished carpenter—recognized as the best in all the surrounding Ozark hills.

When he did a job he seemed to stand back and survey it to see if there was anything left out that could be added to make it as nearly perfect as possible. Then he would see some little place that the average person would pass up and he would be busy touching up this and that. Then, when he had done his best again, he would look it over and a smile of contentment would come over his face.

I suspect he often said to himself, "My work will be my face and my life." I doubt if he often looked in the mirror and noticed that damaged face where each day the cancer bit a mite deeper.

No matter how humble the home he worked in, or how small the job, or how crude the other work around and about, it never seemed to bother him at all. This was his work, and it had to be done right. He appeared never to give a glance at the work of others; a shoddy job done by someone else was not his concern. His own work seemed to be all that mattered. Nevertheless, I suspect when the job was done he had an inner sense of pride and joy when he saw how outstanding it was—but never once did I hear him boast about it.

As the years went by, he became weaker and weaker, his step was less sure, and his hands did not move with the confidence and speed that had so characterized him. He was unable to do many things he had done before. However, no matter what the work or pay, he always had an insatiable desire to do a good job.

The help he was able to get were not able to catch his vision; they thought he was cranky to try so hard to complete each and every detail. So more and more he worked alone. He did not complain or bitterly rail at the inefficiency of the other fellow. He would just appear the next morning by himself with no explanation of the absence of his helper.

During the latter days when he had only the shambles of a face, he would wrap it up in a red bandana handkerchief, leaving only his eyes showing.

When you met him on the street, there was always a cheery greeting. As time went on and he found it more and more difficult to say the words, often his greeting would be given with a move of his walking stick. This stick, too, was a thing of beauty, carved out by his skillful hands.

His life seemed to be filled with contentment and peace. I am sure many times he thanked God for those hands and for the fact that they were marred in no way.

He often would be missed about his usual haunts for weeks, or perhaps months, as he would make his journey to the hospital for the surgeon to cut away a little more. Then you would see him again—a bit more gruesome. There would be no complaint, no telling of his operation and the pain. He would just quietly go about the work that was always awaiting his return.

In all this quarter of a century, I never knew him to come back with any complaints or mention in any way the pain. You would think there was nothing the matter if you did not see his face.

When his days of labor seemed to be coming to an end, his chief concern was that his tools might be in good hands. He sent for me one day and told me that he wished I would find for him some young man who would appreciate and properly use them.

When I took a young man to see him about the tools, there came over his face a look of contentment and satisfaction. His work was finished and he was ready to cash in.

A few days before he died I went to see him. He was walking in the yard. His face was nearly completely covered with bandages and only his eyes were uncovered. As he hobbled about the yard, he said to me, "I am going to keep young just as long as I can."

The day he died I went to see him again. The odor in the room was so offensive you could hardly stay there. What was left of his face was a mass of scars and there was really no longer anything to cut away. You could tell he was in great pain and had many a sleepless night, but still there was no word of complaint.

I shall never forget his last words. Ever afterwards they have made me ashamed whenever I am inclined to complain. Still, day after day, they are vivid in my memory.

These words were: "God has been awfully good to me. I have never had any reason to complain."

R. M. Good

The Custom of the Corn

Long years ago, the historian tells us, our Pilgrim ancestors had the custom of putting five grains of corn upon each empty plate before the Thanksgiving dinner was served. In answer to the questions of the children, their parents explained that their forefathers had come to such dire straits that there was an allowance per person of five grains of corn to eat each day.

A. Ray Grummon

Autumn Sunset

The sun sets on some retired meadow, where no house is visible, with all the glory and splendour that it lavishes on cities; and, perchance, as it has never set before—where there is but a solitary marsh-hawk to have his wings gilded by it, or only a musquash looks out from his cabin, and there is some little black-veined brook in the midst of the marsh, just beginning to meander, winding slowly round a decaying stump. We walked in so pure and bright a light, gilding the withered grass and leaves, so softly and serenely bright, I thought I had never bathed in such a golden flood, without a ripple or a murmur to it. The west side of every wood and rising ground gleamed like a boundary of Elysium, and the sun on our backs seemed like a gentle herdsman driving us home at evening.

So we saunter toward the Holy Land, till one day the sun shall shine more brightly than ever he has done, shall perchance shine into our minds and hearts, and light up our whole lives with a great awakening light, as warm and serene and golden as on a bank-side in autumn.

Henry David Thoreau

Keeping Thanksgiving

There is no hearth so bleak and bare
But heaven hath sent some blessings there.

No table e'er so sparsely spread
But that a grace should there be said.

No life but knows some moment blest
Of sweet contentment and of rest;

No heart so cold but heaven above
Hath touched it with the warmth of love.

So count your blessings, one by one,
At early morn and set of sun,

And, like an incense, to the skies
Your prayers of thankfulness shall rise.

Look for the love that heaven sends,
The good that every soul intends;

Thus you will learn the only way
To keep a true Thanksgiving Day.

Author Unknown

Early Thanksgiving Proclamation

I, George Washington, president of the United States, do recommend to all religious societies and denominations, and to all persons whomsoever, within the United States, to set apart and observe Thursday, the 19th day of February next, as a day of public Thanksgiving and prayer, and on that day to meet together and render sincere and hearty thanks to the great ruler of nations for the manifold and signal mercies which distinguish our lot as a nation, particularly for the possession of constitutions of government which unite, and, by their union, establish liberty with order, for the preservation of peace, foreign and domestic; for a reasonable control which has been given to a spirit of disorder in the suppression of the late insurrection.

And generally for the prosperous condition of our affairs, public and private, and at the same time humbly and fervently beseeech the kind Author of these blessings graciously to prolong them to us; to imprint on our hearts a deep and solemn sense of our obligations to Him for them; to teach us rightly to estimate their immense value; to preserve us from the arrogance of prosperity, and from hazarding the advantages we enjoy by delusive pursuits; to dispose us to merit the continuance of His favors by not abusing them, and by a corresponding conduct as citizens and as men; to render this country more and more a safe and propitious asylum for the unfortunate of other countries; to extend among us true and useful knowledge; to diffuse and establish habits of sobriety, order, morality, piety, and finally to impart all the blessings we possess or ask for ourselves to the whole family of mankind.

In testimony whereof, I have caused the seal of the United States of America to be affixed to these presents, and signed the same with my hand. Done at the city of Philadelphia the first day of January, 1795.

George Washington

A Heart to Praise Thee

Thou hast given so much to me,
Give one thing more—a grateful heart:
Not thankful when it pleaseth me,
As if thy blessings had spare days,
But such a heart whose Pulse may be
Thy Praise.

George Herbert

The Hardest Thanksgiving

If we think deeply, Thanksgiving is always difficult. What is the most difficult aspect of the honored and traditional practice of expressing our appreciation to our God? What is the hardest thanksgiving?

Is it the thanksgiving of affluence? This may seem peculiar. But it is apparent that the more richly blessed we become, the more difficult it becomes for us to be humbly grateful. We are human enough to fall into the plight foreseen in the Deuteronomic history: "Take heed lest you forget the Lord your God, by not keeping his commandments and his ordinances and his statutes . . . lest, when you have eaten and are full, and have built goodly houses and live in them, and when your herds and flocks multiply, and your silver and gold is multiplied, and all that you have is multiplied, then your heart be lifted up, and you forget the Lord your God. . . . [And] you say in your heart, 'My power and the might of my hand have gotten me this wealth' " (Deuteronomy 8:11-17).

It seems so true. We have gotten our houses and automobiles and insurance policies by the power of our own hands. Our affluence is the product of our work, not our worship. In fact, we wonder in secret if God cares whether we have plenty or little. He certainly does not seem to provide for the rest of the world. And He does seem to help those who help themselves. Yes, it is hard to give thanks to God for His blessings (if they really are His) when we have much.

But that is not the hardest thanksgiving.

Well, then, is the hardest thanksgiving that which we make in desolation? Habakkuk's psalm gives an example of this:

> Though the fig tree do not blossom,
> Nor fruit be on the vines,
> the produce of the olive fail,
> and the fields yield no food,
> the flock be cut off from the fold
> and there be no herd in the stalls,
> Yet I will rejoice in the Lord,
> I will joy in the God of my salvation.
> (Habakkuk 3:17-18)

Those old enough to recall the Great Depression know how difficult it is to sing Habakkuk's song on an empty stomach.

But there is more at stake here than hunger. Adversity cuts at self-respect. One woman said, "Oh, we always had something to eat at Thanksgiving time. But all those years I wished just once we could have turkey, not chicken."

An immature view? Of course. Unless you too cannot afford what others have for their children. It is hard to give thanks when you hurt.

How painful was that first Thanksgiving when the family gathered without father, or mother, or wife, or husband, or child. Thanksgiving under adversity is hard, perhaps harder than thanksgiving in affluence.

But that is not the hardest thanksgiving.

In the deepest sense, Christian thanksgiving has relatively little to do with how much or little we have, how great or insignificant our suffering may be, for Christian thanksgiving is not offered chiefly for food and comfort. It is not even for deliverance from suffering.

Christian thanksgiving is for the ever-present grace of God in Jesus Christ. At times God's grace seems more apparent, and we tend to measure it in terms of the presence of money and the absence of medical bills. At other times it is not so.

Christian thanksgiving is that which we offer, not just on Thanksgiving Day, but all year long. It is the thanks expressed in our daily practices, not just our devout prayers; in our dedications, not just our declarations; in our work, not just our works. Or, as the traditional prayer has it, "not with our lips, but with our lives." True thanksgiving is man's total, daily life-response to God's total, eternal grace.

As post-Crucifixion, post-Resurrection Christians, our question is not so grandiose as was the lawyer's, "What shall I do to inherit eternal life?" God's grace has taken care of that.

Our question is much more simple. "How can I show true thanks?" The answer is the same. "You shall love the Lord your God with all your heart, and with all your soul, and with all your strength, and with all your mind; and your neighbor as yourself."

That is the hardest thanksgiving.

George F. Bennett

God's World

O world, I cannot hold thee close enough!
  Thy winds, thy wide gray skies!
  Thy mists, that roll and rise!
Thy woods, this autumn day, that ache and sag
And all but cry with color! That gaunt crag
To crush! To lift the lean of that black bluff!
World, world! I cannot get thee close enough!

Long have I known a glory in it all
  But never knew I this,
  Here such a passion is
As stretcheth me apart. Lord, I do fear
Thou'st made the world too beautiful this year.
My soul is all but out of me—let fall
No burning leaf; prithee, let no bird call.

Edna St. Vincent Millay

For These I Give Thanks

I use two canes when I walk. My vision is blurred and double. When I read a book or a letter, I must concentrate so hard on focusing on each word that I sometimes lose the meaning of what I am reading.

It is very difficult for me to hold a pencil, put a pot on the kitchen stove or even turn the knob on the TV set. I have long given up trying to thread a needle.

I have multiple sclerosis. It is a chronic, crippling disease of the central nervous system. Often, it culminates in paralysis. The symptoms are many and varied: extreme fatigue, loss of balance, slurred speech, loss of bladder and bowel control. An M.S. sufferer may have one or all of these symptoms. Some of my friends are in wheelchairs. Some use leg braces or a supporting frame in order to walk.

When my baby was tiny, I carried him only when absolutely necessary. There were times when I would fall with him in my arms.

I teach piano, but only the theory of it. I had to give up playing because my hands became numb and my legs grew too weak to press the pedal.

I like to do as much housework as I can, but it now takes me six hours to do what I once could do in one.

I am 31 years old. Five years ago I could still do a good day's work. I drove a car, I could swim, bowl, skate. Today, I can do none of these things.

Last summer, I went to the shore and to the zoo with my husband and our little boy. They walked. I rode in a wheelchair.

All this sounds like a letting-go, an indulgence in self-pity.

About an hour ago, this would have been true. I was feeling so sorry for myself, it was sickening. I felt that nobody knew, nobody understood, nobody cared. It was midnight and my melancholy kept me from sleep.

I decided to get up. I had to do something. Anything.

I tiptoed into my baby's room. Here he was, my two-and-a-half-year-old boy, relaxed as a puppy, sleeping so peacefully. I looked down on him for a long time. And suddenly, without really meaning to, I bowed my head in prayer. Help me, I prayed, to overcome this self-pity, for it shuts out those I love and blinds me to my blessings . . .

I had often sung the hymn, *Count Your Many Blessings.* Thinking about it, I almost laughed. Blessings? I had been counting troubles instead. Yet, when it really comes down to it, in counting troubles I could name only one. I have multiple sclerosis. But there is a whole list of blessings.

As I stood, looking at Johnny, I silently asked God to give me the spiritual strength to rise above my one trouble, my physical infirmities.

I kissed my hand and placed it on Johnny's cheek. It felt soft and warm. In this slumber, he grinned his crooked little grin.

I tiptoed out of Johnny's room and returned to my own. There, my husband was sleeping soundly. I thought about the nine wonderful years since our marriage. Surely, we have had our troubles but, as it says in Romans 8:28, "All things work together for good to them that love God . . ."

Again, here was a reason to be grateful.

Once again I left the bedroom and went into the kitchen. There were a few dirty dishes in the sink. My mother and brother and his wife had been over for the evening. We had played a few games, had a few laughs. We'd had some cake and tea. It had been a pleasant evening.

This little family group, I thought to myself, was something else to be grateful for. My father was not with us. He had died 16 years ago. He had been a great dad. Wasn't his memory yet another cause for thankfulness? Another blessing to count?

I wandered out on the back porch. It was peaceful out there. Just a trace of a breeze. A dog barking in the distance. A myriad stars in the sky.

Again I bowed my head.

"Thank you, Lord," I whispered, "for the serenity and quiet of this night."

Sherry Brion Zearfaus

Thanksgiving

For all true words that have been spoken,
For all brave deeds that have been done,
For every loaf in kindness broken,
For every race in valor run,
For martyr lips which have not failed
To give God praise and smile to rest,
For knightly souls which have not quailed
At stubborn strife or lonesome quest;
Lord unto whom we stand in thrall
We give Thee thanks for all, for all.

For each fair field where golden stubble
Hath followed wealth of waving grain;
For every passing wind of trouble
Which bends Thy grass that lifts again;
For gold in mine that men must seek,
For work which bows the sullen knee;
For strength, swift sent to aid the weak,
For love by which we climb to Thee;
Thy freemen, Lord, yet each Thy thrall,
We give Thee praise for all, for all.

Margaret E. Sangster

Truly Great Treasures

He who is young can be thankful that he still has all the exciting experiences of life before him.

He who is old can be thankful that he has attained judgment and understanding and has learned to be tranquil about problems which once troubled him.

He who is in good health can be thankful for a treasure greater than gold.

He who is ill or physically disabled can be thankful for the loving care of family and friends, and for a chance to be an inspiring example of patience and fortitude.

He who dwells in the country can be thankful for the wide open beauty of God's handiwork, where Nature's artistry is manifest on every hand.

He who resides in the city can be thankful for the warmth of human relationships and the opportunity to serve one's fellowman at every turn.

He who has riches of gold and silver can be thankful that life's bounty has given him the privilege and joy of sharing with those less fortunate.

He who is without wordly wealth can be thankful that the truly great treasures of life are free—kindness, friendship, love, appreciation.

He who worships can be thankful that he lives in a country where he may worship according to the dictates of his own conscience.

He who lives in a free country can be thankful that his opportunities are many, and that his chance of success is not hampered by regimentation.

For these things we should be thankful.

As the Years Roll Onward

I learn, as the years roll onward
and leave the past behind,
That much I have counted sorrow
but proves that the world is kind;

That many a flower I longed for
had a hidden thorn of pain,
And many a rugged bypath
led to fields of ripened grain.

For as peace comes after suffering,
and love is reward of pain,
So after earth comes heaven,
and out of our loss the gain.

Author Unknown

Golden Splendor

It's getting on to fall again . . .
The crows begin to call again
And gather in the nearby woods
In strangely busy flocks.
The mist is on the hills once more,
And lavish nature spills once more
A flood of shining gold upon
The humblest of the stocks.

The woods are in their best today,
In bronze and scarlet dressed today,
They seem a patchwork counterpane
Of color and design;
We wake to find at dawn again
Rich diamonds on the lawn again,
For every night's a jeweler
With gems surpassing fine.

Though walk you west or east today
Your eye will have a feast today,
For there is beauty all about
And splendor everywhere;
And it may be when strife is done,
The charm of peace shall settle down
And hide the lines of care.

Oh, always with the fall again,
When beauty covers all again,
The thought returns; If God rewards
The humblest vine and tree,
If splendor crowns their days at last,
Shall we not hear His praise at last,
Shall men not wear a glow of pride
For what they tried to be?

Edgar A. Guest

Worship

The Finding

Flee we to our Lord and we shall be comforted, touch we Him and we shall be made clean, cleave we to Him and we shall be sure, and safe from all manner of peril.

For our courteous Lord willeth that we should be as homely with him as heart may think or soul may desire. But let us beware that we take not so recklessly this homeliness as to leave courtesy. For our Lord Himself is sovereign homeliness, and as homely as He is, so courteous He is: for He is very courteous. And the blessed creatures that shall be in heaven with Him without end, He will have them like to Himself in all things. And to be like our Lord perfectly, it is our very salvation and our full bliss. . . .

God, of Thy Goodness, give me Thyself: for Thou art enough to me, and I may nothing ask that is less than may be full worship to Thee; and if I ask anything that is less, ever me wanteth,—but only in Thee I have all.

Dame Julian of Norwich

The Weaver

My life is but a weaving
  Between my Lord and me,
I cannot choose the colors
  He worketh steadily.

Ofttimes He weaveth sorrow,
  And I in foolish pride
Forget He sees the upper
  And I, the underside.

Not till the loom is silent
  And the shuttles cease to fly
Shall God unroll the canvas
  And explain the reason why.

The dark threads are as needful
  In the Weaver's skillful hand
As the threads of gold and silver
  In the pattern He has planned.

Author Unknown

If He Came to Your House

Would you meet Him at the door with arms outstretched in welcome?
Or would you have to change your clothes before you let Him in?
Or hide some magazines, and put the Bible where they'd been?
Would you hide your worldly music and put some hymn books out?
Could you let Jesus walk right in, or would you rush about?
And I wonder—if the Saviour spent a day or two with you,
Would you go right on doing the things you always do?
Would you go right on saying the things you always say?
Would life for you continue as it does from day to day?
Would you take Jesus with you everywhere you'd planned to go?
Or would you maybe change your plans for just a day or so?
Would you be glad to have Him meet your very closest friends?
Or would you hope they stay away until His visit ends?
Would you be glad to have Him stay forever on and on?
Or would you sigh with great relief when He at last was gone?
It might be interesting to know the things that you would do,
If Jesus came in person to spend some time with you.

Lois Blanchard Eades

There's a Wideness in God's Mercy

There's a wideness in God's mercy,
Like the wideness of the sea;
There's a kindness in his justice,
Which is more than liberty.

There is no place where earth's sorrows
Are more felt than up in heaven;
There is no place where earth's failings
Have such kindly judgment given.

For the love of God is broader
Than the measure of man's mind;
And the heart of the Eternal
Is most wonderfully kind.

If our love were but more simple,
We should take him at his word;
And our lives would be all sunshine
In the sweetness of our Lord.

Frederick W. Faber

Humility

Day by day a voice is asking:

"Without the compulsion of duty and the lure of reward, are you big enough to stoop to serve another's need?

"Are you big enough to fall on your knees in the presence of greatness?

"Are you big enough to play the game when victory seems most hopeless?

"Without envy or jealousy, are you big enough to see another succeed?

"Are you big enough to see something more than sin in the most forlorn of mortals, and something more than vanity in the most highly acclaimed?

"Are you big enough to see the rainbow gleam on the far horizon when all others have been blinded by cynicism and discouragement?

"Are you big enough to endure a blow from both friend and foe, and return for it forgiveness?

"Are you big enough to contemplate 'the great adventure' without fear or regret?

"If you are big enough for this, then you are small enough to be called great, and art become one of God's little children, 'for of such is the kingdom of heaven.'"

Dr. W. Waldemar W. Argow

A Land That Man Has Newly Trod

A land that man has newly trod,
  A land that only God has known,
  Through all the soundless cycles flown.

Yet perfect blossoms bless the sod,
  And perfect birds illume the trees
  And perfect unheard harmonies

Pour out eternally to God.

A thousand miles of mighty wood
  Where thunder-storms stride fireshod;
  A thousand flowers every rod.

A stately tree on every rood,
  Then ten thousand leaves on every tree,
  And each a miracle to me;

And yet there be men who question God!

Joaquin Miller

Growing Old Gracefully

A group of elderly persons recently sat together talking about the art of growing old. One of them returned home and wrote this epitaph for himself, telling how he would like men to remember him: "Here lies an old man who in his ascending years had learned the art of growing old pleasantly. Children loved him, young people sought his company, old people eagerly desired his friendship, and no one ever called him a bore when he had gone out. He knew how to be silent at the right time, and when he spoke he said words that looked more to the future than the past. He was never disturbed because he was not noticed, and he maintained his serenity because he loved God and thought of him more often than he did himself. He lived with optimism for his own times and for what was to follow, and died loving God and man."

Costen J. Harrell

Now and Then

There were hours when life was bitter
With the anguish of defeat,
When strange it seemed that anything
Had ever tasted sweet.
And we scarce knew how to bear it,
But One came o'er the wave,
And the peace He gave us with a word
Then made us strong and brave.

There are hours when work is pressing,
Just little homely work
That must be done, that we must do,
That it were shame to shirk,
And in those hours full often,
To crown the petty cares,
Has fallen upon the house a gleam
Of God's Heaven unawares.

So, for our hallowed hours
We find them, where our Lord
Has called us into service meet
For blessing and reward;
They are sometimes in the closet,
They are often in the mart,
And the Lord can make them anywhere,
His "desert place apart."

Margaret E. Sangster

golden prayers

We seem to give him back to Thee, dear God, who gavest him to us. Yet as Thou didst not lose him in giving, so we have not lost him by his return. Not as the world giveth, givest Thou, O Lover of Souls! What Thou givest Thou takest not away. For what is Thine is ours always, if we are Thine. And life is eternal, and love is immortal, and death is only a horizon, and a horizon is nothing but the limit of our sight. Lift us up, strong Son of God, that we may see farther; cleanse our eyes that we may see more clearly; draw us closer to Thyself that we may know ourselves nearer to our beloved who are with Thee. And while Thou dost prepare a place for us, prepare us for that happy place, that where they are, and Thou art, we too may be. AMEN.

We thank Thee for the dear and faithful dead, for those who have made the distant heavens a Home for us, and whose truth and beauty are even now in our hearts. One by one Thou dost gather the scattered families out of the earthly light into the heavenly glory, from the distractions and strife and weariness of time to the peace of eternity. We thank Thee for the labors and the joys of these mortal years.

Almighty God, comfort us by Thy fullness. Our strength is but weakness, our knowledge is but small, our life but passing away. By Thine eternal wisdom, by Thine unshaken power, Thy constant years, Thine unfailing love, uphold and comfort us, that we, ever feeling that our little lives are altogether in Thee, may look forward to the ending of this mortal life without fear, longing for and hoping for an entrance into that large abundant life where Thou shalt be all in all. AMEN.

George Dawson

The Soul Gathers Force

It is possible, when the future is dim, when our depressed faculties can form no bright ideas of the perfection and happiness of a better world,—it is possible still to cling to the conviction of God's merciful purpose towards His creatures, of His parental goodness even in suffering; still to feel that the path of duty, though trodden with a heavy heart, leads to peace; still to be true to conscience; still to do our work, to resist temptation, to be useful, though with diminished energy, to give up our wills when we cannot rejoice under God's mysterious providence. In this patient, though uncheered obedience, we become prepared for light. The soul gathers force.

W. E. Channing

The One Who Will Meet Your Need

It is not merely that legends have been woven around His name. Every great religious genius has been enhaloed with loving legend. The significant fact is that time has not faded the vividness of His image. Poetry still sings His praise. He is still the living comrade of countless lives.

Dead leaders, no matter how great; dead teachers, no matter how brilliant, cannot fill the longing of a human soul for fellowship with God and freedom from sin. But the crucified, resurrected Christ, living in the presence of God today, can satisfy the deepest longing of the human soul. Have *you* "tasted and seen that the Lord is good"? Come to Christ and find in Him the One who will meet your every need.

In the Morning

I met God in the morning,
When my day was at its best
And His presence came like sunrise
Like a glory in my breast.

All day long the Presence lingered.
All day long He stayed with me.
And we sailed with perfect calmness
O'er a very troubled sea.

Other ships were blown and battered
Other ships were sore distressed.
But the winds that seemed to drive them
Brought to us a peace and rest.

Then I thought of other mornings
With a keen remorse of mind,
When I, too, had loosed the moorings
With the Presence left behind.

So I think I know the secret
Learned from many a troubled way.
You must seek God in the morning
If you want Him through the day.

Ralph Cushman

"Behold I Stand at the Door and Knock"

The famous masterpiece, "The Light of the World," by Holman Hunt depicts Christ standing and knocking at an old vine-covered door. From its dilapidated appearance it is easy to see that it has not been opened in a long time. The Lord holds a lighted lantern and He says, "Behold!" "I stand at the door and knock." When his masterpiece was completed Hunt invited other well-known artists to look at it and give their comments. They were unanimous in their praise and one and all acclaimed it as a masterpiece.

"But," said one, "there is something missing."

"What is that?" asked Hunt.

"A latch on the door."

"No," said Hunt, "I have purposely omitted it. That is the door of the heart and it opens only from within."

Thy Presence

Thy calmness bends serene above
  My restlessness to still;
Around me flows Thy quickening life,
  To nerve my faltering will;
Thy presence fills my solitude;
Thy providence turns all to good.

Samuel Longfellow

Prayer

More things are wrought by prayer
Than this world dreams of. Wherefore, let thy voice
Rise like a fountain for me night and day.
For what are men better than sheep or goats
That nourish a blind life within the brain,
If, knowing God, they lift not hands of prayer
Both for themselves and those who call them friend?
For so the whole round earth is every way
Bound by gold chains about the feet of God.

Alfred Tennyson

GOLDEN NOTES

My Faith Looks Up to Thee

This hymn is America's most important contribution to the hymnody of the Christian Church. It was written in 1830 by Rev. Ray Palmer, D.D. (1808–1887), when he had been graduated from college, but had not yet begun his theological studies. It did not appear until 1832, when it was published in the first part of Mason and Hastings's *Spiritual Songs for Social Worship.* It was Lowell Mason who became its sponsor and set the American Church to singing it, by setting it to music known as "Olivet."

Mason had met Palmer on the street and asked whether he had not a hymn adapted to the former's use. Palmer produced this hymn from a pocketbook and they entered a nearby store to write a copy. Was not that casual meeting on the street a providence? Mason met Palmer a few days later and said to him, "You may live many years, and do many good things, but I think you will be best known to posterity as the author of 'My faith looks up to Thee.' "

My faith looks up to Thee,
Thou Lamb of Calvary,
Saviour divine!
Now hear me while I pray,
Take all my guilt away,
O let me from this day
Be wholly Thine!

May Thy rich grace impart
Strength to my fainting heart,
My zeal inspire;
As Thou hast died for me,
O may my love to Thee
Pure, warm, and changeless be,
A living fire!

While life's dark maze I tread,
And griefs around me spread,
Be Thou my Guide;
Bid darkness turn to day,
Wipe sorrow's tears away,
Nor let me ever stray
From Thee aside.

When ends life's transient dream,
When death's cold, sullen stream
Shall o'er me roll;
Blest Saviour, then, in love,
Fear and distrust remove;
O bear me safe above,
A ransomed soul! AMEN.

This hymn has been sung all around the world, in Tamil, Tahitian, Arabic, Rhu, Chinese—in every language where Christian missionaries are labouring.

The hymn is purely personal experience with the whole Bible back of it, and not based on merely an isolated passage.

The first verse portrays the penitent sinner praying that his guilt might be taken away and asking that he might be accepted by the "Lamb of Calvary." The second pleads for needed grace and zeal and love to Christ, that his newly won salvation might become in him "a living fire." The third asks for guidance amid darkness, grief and sorrow, that the soul may never stray "from Thee aside." The fourth foresees the hour of culmination of the soul's spiritual endeavour and urges, "Oh, bear me safe above, A ransomed soul," making a very satisfying climax to this cry of the developing soul.

Dr. Palmer's character gave the spirit to his hymns. An intimate friend said of him to Dr. Benson: "One of the loveliest of men. There was a certain saintliness in his manner and personality. He was gentle in his ways of speech, but had very deep feelings which often came to the surface in conversation."

Dr. Palmer carried the hymn about with him in his little pocketbook and it took Lowell Mason to get it out into public use. Then it appeared anonymously in the American religious press where it was found by Rev. Andrew Reed and used in his *Hymn-book.* Thus it started out on both sides of the sea on its mission of deepening religious experience and comforting the weak in faith.

The hymn was a transcript of young Palmer's personal experience. "It was in an hour when Christ, in the riches of His grace and love, was so vividly apprehended as to fill the soul with deep emotion that the piece was composed. There was not the slightest thought of writing for another eye, least of all of writing a hymn for Christian worship. . . . It is well remembered that when writing the last line, 'A ransomed soul,' the thought that the whole work of redemption and salvation was involved in those words, and suggested the theme of eternal praises, moved the writer to a degree of emotion that brought abundant tears."—*Dr. Ray Palmer in an appendix to his "Poetical Works."*

GOLDEN THOUGHTS

Closer is He than breathing, nearer than hands and feet.

Alfred Tennyson

Our God is at home with the rolling spheres, and at home with broken hearts.

N. P. Ferguson

We shall steer safely through every storm, so long as our heart is right, our intention fervent, our courage steadfast, and our trust fixed on God.

Author Unknown

Daily Supply

"The inward man is renewed day by day" (II Cor. 4:16). A man can no more take in a supply of grace for the future than he can eat enough today to last him for the next six months, or take sufficient air into his lungs at once to sustain life for a week to come. We must draw upon God's boundless stores for grace from day to day, as we need it.

Dwight L. Moody

Just for Today

Lord, for tomorrow and its needs
I do not pray:
Keep me, my God, from stain of sin
Just for today.

Let me both diligently work
And duly pray,
Let me be kind in word and deed
Just for today.

Let me be slow to do my will,
Prompt to obey,
Help me to mortify my flesh
Just for today.

Let me no wrong or idle word
Unthinking say:
Set Thou a seal upon my lips
Just for today.

And if today my tide of life
Should ebb away,
Give me Thy sacraments divine,
Sweet Lord, today.

So for tomorrow and its needs
I do not pray
But keep me, guide me, love me, Lord.
Just for today.

Sybil F. Partridge

A Gift of Light

In Paris, a woman who was poor and blind once put twenty-seven francs into an offering plate.

"But you cannot afford so much," said her friend.

"Yes, I can," she answered.

When pressed to explain, she said, "I am blind and I asked my fellow straw-workers how much they spent in a year for oil for their lamps when it is too dark to work. They told me, twenty-seven francs.

"So," said the blind woman, "I found out that I save so much in a year because I am blind and do not need a lamp to work, and I give it to shed light to the dark, *heathen* lands."

D. Luben

Sheer Joy

Oh the sheer joy of it!
  Living with Thee,
God of the universe,
  Lord of a tree,
Maker of mountains,
  Lover of me!

Oh the sheer joy of it!
  Breathing Thy air;
Morning is dawning,
  Gone every care,
All the world's singing,
  "God's everywhere."

Oh the sheer joy of it!
  Walking with Thee,
Out on the hilltop,
  Down by the sea,
Life is so wonderful,
  Life is so free.

Oh the sheer joy of it!
  Ever to be
Living in glory,
  Living with Thee,
Lord of tomorrow,
  Lover of me!

Ralph Spaulding Cushman

God Does Do Such Wonderful Things!

God does do such wonderful things!
How can we doubt He'll see us through?
He has proved Himself through a million springs,
Yet still we wonder: "What shall we do?"
The world is black with war and woe—
But look where the pussy willows grow,
And hear the songs and see the wings . . .
God does do such wonderful things!

Angela Morgan

Pray remember what I have recommended to you, which is, to think often on God, by day, by night, in your business, and even in your diversions. He is always near you and with you; leave Him not alone. You would think it rude to leave a friend alone who came to visit you: why then must God be neglected? Do not then forget Him, but think on Him often, adore Him continually, live and die with Him; this is the glorious employment of a Christian; in a word, this is our profession; if we do not know it we must learn it. I will endeavour to help you with my prayers.

A letter of Brother Lawrence

Pilgrimage

So long I have been guided by Thy power
Up many a tangled path and stony hill,
And now, dear Lord, through this strange darkened hour
Be with me still.

Be with me, for the way is long and lonely,
I am bewildered, and I cannot see,
But, Lord, I shall not be afraid if only
You walk with me.

If I can ever keep recalling
The darkened roads I traveled in the past,
How, after You long guarded me from falling,
Light shone at last:

Then surely, Lord, I can go forward knowing
That somewhere on the hills the light will dawn,
And I shall reach it safely if, in going,
You still lead on.

Grace Noll Crowell

God's Sand Is Gold

If one should give me a dish of sand, and tell me there were particles of iron in it, I might look for them with my eyes, and search for them with my clumsy fingers, and be unable to detect them; but let me take a magnet and sweep through it, and how it would draw to itself the almost invisible particles by the mere power of attraction. — The unthankful heart, like my finger in the sand, discovers no mercies; but let the thankful heart sweep through the day, and as the magnet finds the iron, so it will find, in every hour, some heavenly blessings, only the iron in God's sand is gold!

Henry Ward Beecher

My Spirit Longeth for Thee

My spirit longeth for Thee,
Within my troubled breast
Altho' I be unworthy
Of so divine a Guest.

Of so divine a Guest,
Unworthy tho' I be,
Yet has my heart no rest,
Unless it come from Thee.

Unless it come from Thee,
In vain I look around;
In all that I can see,
No rest is to be found.

No rest is to be found,
But in Thy blessed love;
O! let my wish be crown'd,
And send it from above!

John Byrom

If I Have Faltered More or Less

If I have faltered more or less
In my great task of happiness;
If I have moved among my race
And shown no glorious morning face;
If beams from happy eyes
Have moved me not; if morning skies,
Books, and my food, and Summer rain
Knocked on my sullen heart in vain: —
Lord, Thy most pointed pleasure take
And stab my spirit broad awake.

Robert Louis Stevenson

Dear Lord and Father of Mankind

Dear Lord and Father of mankind!
  Forgive our foolish ways!
Reclothe us in our rightful mind,
In purer lives Thy service find,
  In deeper reverence, praise.

In simple trust like theirs who heard,
  Beside the Syrian sea,
The gracious calling of the Lord,
Let us, like them, without a word,
  Rise up and follow Thee.

O Sabbath rest by Galilee!
  O calm of hills above,
Where Jesus knelt to share with Thee
The silence of eternity
  Interpreted by love!

With that deep hush subduing all
  Our words and works that drown
The tender whisper of Thy call,
As noiseless let Thy blessing fall
  As fell Thy manna down.

Drop Thy still dews of quietness,
  Till all our strivings cease;
Take from our souls the strain and stress,
And let our ordered lives confess
  The beauty of Thy peace.

Breathe through the heats of our desire
  Thy coolness and Thy balm;
Let sense be dumb, let flesh retire;
Speak through the earthquake, wind and fire,
  O still small voice of calm!

John Greenleaf Whittier

The Burning Bush

I will now turn aside and see this great sight.—EXODUS 3:3

Thy wisdom and Thy might appear,
Eternal God, through every year;
From day to day, from hour to hour,
Thy works reveal self-ordered power.

We worship Thee whose will hath laid
Thy sovereign rule on all things made;
The faithful stars, the fruitful earth,
Obey Thy laws that gave them birth.

Yet Thou canst make a marvel shine
Amid these mighty laws of Thine,
As when Thy servant Moses came
And saw the bush with Thee aflame.

We turn aside and tread the ways
That lead through wonder up to praise;
Wherever Thou by man art found
The homely earth is holy ground.

If Thou hast formed us out of dust
Through ages long,—in Thee we trust;
O grant us in our souls to see
The living flame that comes from Thee.

Henry van Dyke

What God Hath Promised

God hath not promised
  Skies always blue,
Flower-strewn pathways
  All our lives through;
God hath not promised
  Sun without rain,
Joy without sorrow,
  Peace without pain.

But God hath promised
  Strength for the day,
Rest for the labor,
  Light for the way,
Grace for the trials,
  Help from above,
Unfailing sympathy,
  Undying love.

Annie Johnson Flint

Psalm Eight

O Lord our Lord, how excellent is Thy name in all the earth! Who hast set Thy glory above the heavens.

Out of the mouth of babes and sucklings hast Thou ordained strength because of Thine enemies, that Thou mightest still the enemy and the avenger.

When I consider Thy heavens, the work of Thy fingers, the moon and the stars, which Thou hast ordained;

What is man, that Thou art mindful of him? And the son of man, that Thou visitest him?

For Thou hast made him a little lower than the angels, and hast crowned him with glory and honour.

Thou madest him to have dominion over the works of Thy hands; Thou hast put all things under his feet:

All sheep and oxen, yea, and the beasts of the field;

The fowl of the air, and the fish of the sea, and whatsoever passeth through the paths of the seas.

O Lord our Lord, how excellent is Thy name in all the earth!

Christmas

Keeping Christmas

It is a good thing to observe Christmas day. The mere marking of times and seasons, when men agree to stop work and make merry together, is a wise and wholesome custom. It helps one to feel the supremacy of the common life over the individual life. It reminds a man to set his own little watch, now and then, by the great clock of humanity which runs on sun time.

But there is a better thing than the observance of Christmas Day, and that is, keeping Christmas.

Are you willing to forget what you have done for other people, and to remember what other people have done for you; to ignore what the world owes you, and to think what you owe the world; to put your rights in the background, and your duties in the middle distance, and your chances to do a little more than your duty in the foreground; to see that your fellow men are just as real as you are, and try to look behind their faces to their hearts, hungry for joy; to own that probably the only good reason for your existence is not what you are going to get out of life, but what are you going to give to life; to close your book of complaints against the management of the universe, and look around you for a place where you can sow a few seeds of happiness—are you willing to do these things even for a day? Then you can keep Christmas.

Are you willing to stoop down and consider the needs and desires of little children; to remember the weakness and loneliness of people who are growing old; to stop asking how much your friends love you, and ask yourself whether you love them enough; to bear in mind the things that other people have to bear in their hearts; to try to understand what those who live in the same house with you really want; without waiting for them to tell you; to trim your lamp so that it will give more light and less smoke, and to carry it in front so that your shadow will fall behind you; to make a grave for your ugly thoughts and a garden for your kindly feelings, with the gate open—are you willing to do these things even for a day? Then you can keep Christmas.

Are you willing to believe that love is the strongest thing in the world—stronger than hate, stronger than evil, stronger than death—and that the blessed life which began in Bethlehem nineteen hundred years ago is the image and brightness of the Eternal Love? Then you can keep Christmas.

And if you keep it for a day, why not always? But you can never keep it alone.

Henry van Dyke

To You

If I could do whate'er I want to do,
To make complete your gladsome Christmas Day,
I would not bring a single thing to you,
But I would come and take some things away:

I'd take away all trouble from your heart;
Each pain and sorrow I would have relieved;
And every word that caused a single smart,
And every hour through which you sadly grieved.

I'd have them all be gone — forever gone —
Forgotten, like the things that cannot be;
And then each hour would be a joyful one,
For only good things would be left, you see.

Now that is what I'd really like to do —
If I could do the things I wish for you.

Author Unknown

Long, Long Ago

Winds through the olive trees
  Softly did blow,
Round little Bethlehem
  Long, long ago.

Sheep on the hillside lay
  Whiter than snow,
Shepherds were watching them,
  Long, long ago.

Then from the happy sky,
  Angels bent low
Singing their song of joy,
  Long, long ago.

For in a manger bed,
  Cradled we know,
Christ came to Bethlehem,
  Long, long ago.

Anonymous

Christmas Comes But Once a Year

God grant ye joy this Christmas day,
May every heart be jolly;
Love kiss ye now beneath the bough
Of mistletoe and holly.
The long hard year of toil is done,
Today the bells are ringing,
Put down your burdens every one
And share the carol singing.

For Christmas comes but once a year,
When harvesting is ended;
With merry din, the day comes in,
By love and mirth attended;
The children dance and shout with glee,
The eyes of all are beaming,
And high above the Christmas tree
The Star of Hope is gleaming.

So homeward turn your steps once more,
And give a kiss to mother,
Let horn and bell the glad news tell
Of each returning brother;
For man has conquered time and space
Regardless of the weather,
And Christmas Day, by God's good grace,
Should find us all together!

Edgar A. Guest

GOLDEN NOTES

Christina Georgina Rossetti was born in London, England, in 1830. Her father was an Italian who had sought refuge in England and became a professor of languages at King's College, London. Her brilliant brother Gabriel has often portrayed his sister's sweet face in his famous paintings of "The Virgin."

The family had to struggle for its existence. Mrs. Rossetti bravely opened a day school for girls; her daughters had to keep the school going. However, owing to a dearth of pupils, this venture did not last very long.

Christina was engaged to be married but, unhappily, the match was broken off on religious grounds. From this time on her gentle spirit was almost overcome by mental suffering. She shut herself into herself more and more, writing many books—about eight in all.

Deeply religious, she was known as a saint and a great poet. The poor children were her friends. In every possible way she gave of herself and her substance to their welfare. One day, in 1872, she wrote this Christmas carol especially for her Sunday school class of the very poor who understood how bleak and cold the winters were:

In the Bleak Mid-winter

In the bleak mid-winter,
  Frosty wind made moan,
Earth stood hard as iron,
  Water like a stone;
Snow had fallen, snow on snow,
  Snow on snow
In the bleak mid-winter
  Long ago.

Our God, heaven cannot hold Him,
  Nor earth sustain;
Heaven and earth shall flee away,
  When he comes to reign;
In the bleak mid-winter,
  A stable-place sufficed
The Lord God Almighty,
  Jesus Christ.

Angels and Archangels
  May have gathered there,
Cherubim and Seraphim
  Thronged the air;
But only his mother,
  In her maiden bliss,
Worshipped the Beloved
  With a kiss.

What can I give Him,
  Poor as I am?
If I were a shepherd,
  I would bring a lamb;
If I were a wise man,
  I would do my part;
Yet what I can I give Him—
  Give my heart.

From *Stories of Beautiful Hymns* by Kathleen Blanchard

Christmas Comfort

Many people need comfort today. Maybe you do.

Like the young woman up the street whose husband has just died, leaving her with three little ones.

Like two dear old ladies of my acquaintance, the last of their family, often given to wondering, and worrying, as to which will go first.

Like Martha, heartsick and weary, her marriage seemingly shattered beyond repair.

Like the little woman in the bungalow on the corner who asks, "What is my boy doing tonight?" The poor soul is a prey to torment and anxiety.

Like Jane, waiting pathetically for Peter and his paycheck, but with slim hopes. He must pass the "Blue Boar" between the factory and his front gate, and he can't resist the temptation.

Like Peter himself, knowing what he should be, knowing what he could be, and in his better moments regretting what he is and wishing miserably that he could give up the wasteful habit.

Indeed, none of us is exempt from some kind of worry. We are all in need of encouragement.

For which reason we can rejoice exceedingly this Christmastime; for if there is one story above all others that is charged with encouragement, it is that of our Saviour's birth when He whose name is "Wonderful Counselor, The Mighty God, The everlasting Father, The Prince of Peace" left the realms of glory and lay helpless, a Babe in mother Mary's arms, His court the creatures of the stable, His cot their crude manger.

Have you read it lately, that story? Read it, I mean, for yourself.

Right there in the center of it you will find the comforting words especially appropriate for you.

For you, whoever you are, borne down under a load of doubt and uncertainty.

For you, so lone and sore bereft, your dearest gone, your future dark.

For you, heart-heavy mothers and fathers, to whom all things have lost their savor while the boy wanders or the girl takes the wrong road.

For you, so many of you, who feel that your tasks are more than one mind can compass or one pair of hands accomplish, your burden more than one pair of shoulders can very well bear.

For you who are worried and perplexed.

For you who are harassed and driven.

For you who are in any kind of need or trouble.

You will find the story in the first two chapters of the Gospel according to Matthew, and in the second chapter of the Gospel according to Luke. It is Matthew who tells us about the visit of the wise men, while Luke tells us about the shepherds. Read both records. There is no detail that is not worth recalling, and every reminder that events were thus and so for the reason that "it might be fulfilled which was spoken by the prophets" cannot but strengthen and confirm our faith.

Especially, however, read the words of the angel to the shepherds, who, Luke tells us, "were sore afraid."

Afraid—like us sometimes—afraid of the future, afraid of our own reactions, afraid because of our weaknesses, afraid for our loved ones, afraid of life's complexities, afraid to hold up our heads, unable to forget.

"Fear not," said the angel: "for, behold, I bring you good tidings of great joy, which shall be to all people. For unto you is born this day . . . a Saviour."

"Unto *us* a Child is born, unto *us* a Son is given: and the government shall be upon *His* shoulder."

What a Child! What a Son! What a shoulder!

To you and me is born a Saviour, and that involves salvation not only in the great Messianic sense, the defeat of the last enemy, the downfall of the great adversary, and the final translation of His people at the time of His second coming; it means salvation *now*, in our daily extremities and perplexities.

It means the acquisition of power to overcome if we will but ask for it and take it. It means the provision of light for our next step.

It means a Rock to lean upon in the day of sudden shock and calamity. It means strength to bear sorrow. It means companionship in our day of loss.

It means that, however bleak the future, we can still go forward dauntless and unafraid, because He, the Saviour, has promised, "As thy days, so shall thy strength be." It means that no matter how hard the task, we may attack it with courage, knowing that with our hands within His hands nothing is beyond our powers.

Best of all, it means that we cannot escape Him. Having done so much, left heaven as He did, lived as He did, suffered as He did, died as He did, He is not going to be bilked of His reward unless we refuse to accept Him. The way we worry and fret sometimes would seem to suggest that we are apprehensive that the Lord will lose interest and stop short, as it were, when He has already gone to such lengths.

As though He would. As though He could.

He tells us that we are the apple of His eye; that we are engraved on the palms of His hands.

Having gone to the uttermost, He will also continue to do the uttermost, right to the very end.

His birth in Bethlehem was a pledge and guarantee that His followers need fear nothing.

The Sacred Word is redolent with "comfortable" words, but these in the heart of the Christmas story embody them all. They are indeed "tidings of great joy." "Unto you," whoever you are, wherever you are, whatever your circumstances or condition, "Unto *you* is born this day . . . a Saviour."

Heaven be praised!

Mary J. Vine

Christmas Meditation

Suppose that Christ had not been born that far-away Judean morn.

Suppose that God, whose mighty hand created worlds, had never planned a way for man to be redeemed.

Suppose the Wise Men only dreamed that guiding star whose light still glows down through the centuries. Suppose Christ never walked here in men's sight, our blessed Way, and Truth and Light.

Suppose He counted all the cost, and never cared that we were lost, and never died for you and me, nor shed His blood on Calvary upon a shameful cross. Suppose that having died, He never rose, and there was none with power to save our souls from death beyond the grave!

As far as piteous heathen know, these things that I've "supposed"—are so.

Martha Snell Nicholson

Christmas Bells

I heard the bells on Christmas Day
Their old familiar carols play,
And wild and sweet
The words repeat,
Of "Peace on earth, good will to men!"

And thought how, as the day had come,
The belfries of all Christendom
Had rolled along
The unbroken song,
Of "Peace on earth, good will to men!"

And in despair I bowed my head;
"There is no peace on earth," I said,
"For hate is strong
And mocks the song
Of Peace on earth, good will to men!"

Then pealed the bells more loud and deep:
"God is not dead; nor doth He sleep!
The wrong shall fail,
The right prevail,
With peace on earth, good will to men!"

Henry Wadsworth Longfellow

How The Great Guest Came

Before the cathedral in grandeur rose
At Ingelburg where the Danube goes;
Before its forest of silver spires
Went airily up to the clouds and fires;
Before the oak had already a beam,
While yet the arch was stone and dream—
There where the altar was later laid,
Conrad, the cobbler, plied his trade.

It happened one day at the year's white end—
Two neighbors called on their old-time friend;
And they found the shop, so meager and mean,
Made gay with a hundred boughs of green.
Conrad was stitching with face ashine,
But suddenly stopped as he twitched a twine;
"Old friends, good news! At dawn today,
As the cocks were scaring the night away,
The Lord appeared in a dream to me,
and said, "I am coming your Guest to be!"
So I've been busy with feet astir,
Strewing the floor with branches of fir.
The wall is washed and the shelf is shined,
And over the rafter the holly twined.
He comes today, and the table is spread.
With milk and honey and wheaten bread".

His friends went home; and his face grew still
As he watched for the shadow across the sill.
He lived all the moments o'er and o'er,
When the Lord should enter the lowly door—
The knock, the call, the latch pulled up,
The lighted face, the offered cup.
He would wash the feet where the spikes had been
He would kiss the hands where the nails went in,
And then at the last would sit with Him
And break the bread as the day grew dim.

While the cobbler mused there passed his pane
A beggar drenched by the driving rain.
He called him in from the stony street
And gave him shoes for his bruised feet.
The beggar went and there came a crone,
Her face with wrinkles of sorrow sewn.
A bundle of faggots bowed her back,
And she was spent with the wrench and rack.
He gave her his loaf and steadied her load
As she took her way on the weary road.
Then to his door came a little child,
Lost and afraid in the world so wild,
In the big, dark world. Catching it up
He gave it the milk in the waiting cup.
And let it home to its mother's arms,
Out of the reach of the world's alarms.

The day went down in the crimson west
And with it the hope of the blessed Guest,
And Conrad sighed as the world turned gray:
"Why is it, Lord, that your feet delay?
Did you forget that this was the day?"
Then soft in the silence a Voice he heard:
"Lift up your heart, for I kept my word.
Three times I came to your friendly door;
Three times my shadow was on your floor.
I was the beggar with bruised feet;
I was the woman you gave to eat;
I was the child on the nameless street.

Edwin Markham

The Meaning of Christmas

Holiday and Holy Day, Christmas is more than a yule log, holly or tree. It is more than natural good cheer and the giving of gifts. Christmas is even more than the feast of the home and of children, the feast of love and friendship. It is more than all these together. Christmas is Christ, the Christ of justice and charity, of freedom and peace.

The joy of Christmas is a joy that war cannot kill, for it is the joy of the soul and the soul cannot die. Poverty cannot prevent the joy of Christmas, for it is a joy no earthly wealth can give. Time cannot wither Christmas, for it belongs to eternity. The world cannot shatter it, for it is union with Him who has overcome the world.

The leaders and peoples of nations must understand these fundamental truths if we are ever to have freedom and peace. Unless charters and pacts have a divine sanction, unless "God is the Paramount Ruler of the world," then again and again, as the waves upon the shore, must catastrophe follow catastrophe. Not until men lay aside greed, hatred, pride and the tyranny of evil passions, to travel the road that began at Bethlehem, will the Star of Christmas peace illuminate the world. Christmas is the Birthday of freedom, *for it is only the power of Christ that makes men free.*

Francis Spellman

A Prayer for Christmas

God give us eyes this Christmas
to see the Christmas Star,
And give us ears to hear the song
of angels from afar . . .
And, with our eyes and ears attuned
for a message from above,
Let "Christmas Angels" speak to us
of hope and faith and love . . .
Hope to light our pathway
when the way ahead is dark,
Hope to sing through stormy days
with the sweetness of the lark,
Faith to trust in things unseen
and know beyond all seeing
That it is in our Father's Love
we live and have our being,
And Love to break down barriers
of color, race, and creed,
Love to see and understand
and help all those in need.

Helen Steiner Rice

The Book That Converted Its Author

The balconies are crowded. Every eye is on the chariots in the great arena below as they speed faster and faster around the course. Will Ben-Hur win? Or will Messala triumph? People are shouting, screaming as the beautiful horses dash into the final stretch.

What a thrilling scene the chariot race in *Ben-Hur* is! In fact, the entire book is an exciting, absorbing story of life in the time of Christ. Though Ben-Hur is the hero, the figure of Christ is always in the background, never forgotten.

Yet *Ben-Hur: A Tale of the Christ* was not written by a religious man. The author, Lew Wallace, had been a soldier, a lawyer, a governor. When he began his famous book, he did not know what he believed about religion. He did not even know whether he believed in Christ. In fact, he began writing the book in an effort to learn for himself the truth about Jesus of Nazareth.

After his active years of service through the Civil War, General Lew Wallace returned to private life and his law practice in Crawfordsville, Indiana. For some time he was restless—the natural reaction from the excitement of war. But at last he settled down to an uneventful life.

Unaccountably, he found himself thinking about religion, although he had no religious convictions whatever. He was particularly haunted by the chapter in the Gospel of St. Matthew which relates the birth of Jesus and the visit of the Wise Men. Who were the Wise Men, he wondered? Where had they come from, and why?

And so, after much reading and study of the Bible, Wallace wrote an account of the meeting of the Magi in the desert, and their journey to Bethlehem to see the Christ-child. When it was finished, he left the manuscript on his desk, undecided what to do with it.

Some time later, on a night in 1876, Wallace was returning home after an evening with friends. He had been listening to a discussion of religion—of God, Jesus, heaven, and eternal life. Wallace had taken little or no part in the argument, for the very good reason that he knew nothing at all about the subject under discussion. Did he believe in God? He did not know. Was Jesus Christ divine? He did not know. Religion had had no place in his active life, and he was totally ignorant about theology.

As he walked home alone in the darkness that evening, Lew Wallace began to regret that ignorance. For the first time in his life he began to feel that religion might be a very important matter. He should believe *something*. But what? How did one find out what to believe? Read sermons? Read theology, on which no two men agreed? No, he would never come to any decision that way. The only thing to do was to read the Bible. As the Bible was the basis for all Christian theology, he would make it the basis for his own religious convictions.

But Wallace knew from experience that he would have to have some definite purpose in studying the Bible—something to keep him at it, to keep him interested. He was not a man to study just for the sake of studying. The search for religious convictions alone would not be enough. He needed something else.

For days Wallace mulled the matter over. Then one day an inspiration came. He went to his wife in great excitement.

"My dear, I'm going to write a book."

"That is splendid," she replied. "I'm glad you are going to start another book. You enjoyed so much your work on *The Fair God.* What will it be this time?"

"A tale of the Christ," Wallace answered. "I shall use what I wrote about the Wise Men as the beginning of the book, and I shall end with the crucifixion. In between—"

"Yes," prompted his wife. "In between—?"

"Well, I hardly know yet. It will be a story which will show the religious and political condition of the world at the time of Christ."

"But will you have Jesus himself in your story?" asked his wife, troubled. "Won't that be dangerous? I'm afraid you will offend many readers who have their own conception of Christ and will not like to see him pictured differently."

Lew Wallace frowned. "That is one of the greatest obstacles I shall have to hurdle," he agreed. "The only solution I can see at present is to have a human hero, who is the central figure in the story. The figure of Christ must be in the background. Yet He must dominate the book. Well, I shan't worry too much about that just yet. I shall be working on this project a long time, no doubt, and many of my difficulties may smooth themselves out before I come to them."

Wallace was right: he worked on his book a long time. More than seven years. Most of the time was taken up with research.

And of course, to make his progress even slower, he had to make a living. Writing was merely spare-time work for him. He was in those years, to begin with, a lawyer, busy enough to suit any man. And then, in 1878, with his book far from finished, he was made governor of the territory of New Mexico. Then, indeed, Wallace knew what it was to be busy. Trying simultaneously to manage a legislature of jealous factions, to take care of an Indian war, and to sell some mines which had been located by the Spanish conquistadors, he found it increasingly difficult to finish his book. Sometimes he could not even start to write before midnight. To cap the climax, in the last months of his work on *Ben-Hur,* he knew that his life was in constant danger. "Billy the Kid" had sworn to kill him.

But Lew Wallace was not a man to let either the pressure of work or the fear of death keep him from finishing what he had started. Patiently, tirelessly he labored. And at last his book was completed and carefully copied in purple ink. His work was done. Not only that, he had discovered, himself, what he wanted: religious convictions. Lew Wallace, in writing his book of the Christ, had come to believe in Him.

Elizabeth Rider Montgomery

Christmas Wish

May you, wherever you are in this golden hour, know joy.
May your hearthfire be surrounded with those near and dear to you;
May the happiness of your children re-echo the gladness heaven sent forth in this time of the Miracle of Bethlehem.

May the faith the humble shepherds found in the starlit stable be yours in fullest measure;
May the exultation of Mary and Joseph light your heart with the glow of divine love.

May you gather together in a bright bouquet, love, charity, and tranquility of spirit,
For he who possesses these holds the key to riches beyond measure.

May all your dreams in this splendid hour reach fulfillment,
And may all the paths you walk be lighted with peace, not only today, but in all the days of the year to come.

Author Unknown

Who Is This

Who is this so weak and helpless,
Child of lowly Hebrew maid,
Rudely in a stable sheltered,
Coldly in a manger laid?

'Tis the Lord of all creation,
Who this wondrous path hath trod,
He is God from everlasting,
And to everlasting God.

Who is this that hangeth dying
While the rude world scoffs and scorns,
Numbered with the malefactors,
Torn with nails, and crowned with thorns?

'Tis our God, our glorious Savior,
Who above the starry sky
Now for us a place prepareth,
Where no tear can dim the eye.

William Walsham How

Our Son Left Us at Christmas

I wasn't thinking about Christmas that hot July morning in 1949, even though seven-year-old Harold had teased for a "bike from Santa" again at breakfast. For the hundredth time I said "Maybe," meaning "No, we can't afford it."

I was in the kitchen getting lunch when I heard shouts in the backyard. Looking out the window, I saw the neighborhood gang. Then I saw my Harold in the midst of them, holding his head. I put my arm around Harold and brought him into the kitchen. Then I bathed the small cut on his forehead and bandaged it. After a day or two I realized the cut wasn't healing the way it should. "Why not take him to the doctor on the next block?" his father suggested.

Next day the doctor looked at the cut, smiled at me over Harold's dark hair, and said, "Nothing but a scratch, Mrs. Balben; I'll dress it for you. And if it'll make you any happier, I'll X-ray his head in the bargain."

Two days later the doctor called me on the phone. He sounded gruff and in a hurry. "Can you stop by this afternoon?" he asked. "You needn't bring Harold," he added.

"Not bring Harold? That's funny," I thought. I thought it even more odd that the doctor should close his office door so carefully behind me. Finally he looked at me. "Mrs. Balben," he said, "there's something very wrong with your son's head."

Then, as I dug my nails into the shiny leather arms of his chair, he told me about a boy's brain and all the diseases that can cripple it. But what he said that afternoon added up to this—something was wrong with Harold's brain and he must be operated on immediately. I've tried to forget those sleepless nights when he was in the hospital; nights when his father and I said to each other, "Everything's going to be all right." We prayed, confused and embarrassed prayers, because we hadn't talked to God for a long time.

On August 19th he went to the operating room of one of the finest hospitals in the country. Within hours, we had our diagnosis. Our son had cancer of the brain and there was no hope. Harold couldn't live till Christmas, the doctors told us. I tried to pray again, but I couldn't. "God," I said bitterly, "Christmas is a time to give, not to take away." Then I asked myself, "But what do I really know of God or heaven, anyway?" Suddenly I realized that perhaps my small son knew more about heaven than I did. I remembered the day, two or three years ago, when he and his brother and sisters had started off to Sunday school for the first time. A neighborhood boy teased me to let them go with him to the Sunday school down the street. From that first day on Harold and the others went every Sunday. I remembered, too, when he had enrolled as a Junior Soldier the previous spring.

"It means that I accept Jesus as my Saviour," he explained. "I signed this." He showed me a pledge: "I have recognized myself to be a sinner, and forsaking my sins I am now trusting in the Lord Jesus Christ as my own Saviour, and I believe that His blood does cleanse me from sin. I will strive by His help to live as His loving and obedient child all my life, and to be His faithful soldier," I read.

Then I remembered how he talked about heaven. His Sunday school teacher told her class about heaven so often that Harold talked about meeting Jesus there as if it were as close as the next town. "Heaven must be a swell place," he'd say.

Three weeks after the doctors had told us about Harold, he came home from the hospital. He looked pale and every so often he touched the bandage on his head in bewilderment. But he remembered:

"Can I have a bike, Ma?" he teased almost every day. "Can I have a bike for Christmas?" Saying no was harder than ever, but how could I pay doctors' bills and still buy a bicycle?

For a while, his father and I demanded that God save our boy. At first we believed He would. But as Harold weakened, we knew the doctors were right, that he couldn't live much longer. I grew more and more bitter. Yet, at the same time, I knew that I had to tell Harold he was going away soon to be with the Jesus he loved.

One afternoon I sat down by his bed to do my mending. "May I, please, please, have a bike when I get well?" he teased. I kept on with my mending, but I said very slowly, "Harold, what would you say if I told you that instead of getting well, you're going away forever, that you're going to heaven to see Jesus?"

He lay back on his pillows and was very still for a second. "Heaven?" he said. "Will I have a new bike there?"

"Yes, Harold," I told him, "you're going to heaven pretty soon and you'll have a golden bicycle when you get there."

He grinned, "Oh, boy," he said, "heaven is wonderful. I heard all about it in Sunday school. Jesus'll be there."

Soon after that, we took him to the hospital.

Since Harold's operation, his Sunday school friends and teacher had been in and out of the house day after day. When I met them next at the hospital, I told them what I had said to Harold about heaven and his golden bike.

"Maybe I did wrong," I said hesitantly.

Next day they called me. "We're going to give Harold his bike here and now," they said.

"We're going to give him the biggest Christmas party he's ever seen, right now."

In the next week, they canvassed the local stores. To sales girls and store managers they told our Harold's story and how he'd never see another Christmas. Within one week he collected footballs, candy, and yes, a red and white tricycle.

On November 19, almost three months to the day after his trip to the operating room, Harold had his Christmas party. We met Harold's Sunday school teacher and friends at the hospital. We were all carrying presents wrapped in gay paper. When we came to his door, Harold tried to smile. Then he saw his bike. He hadn't spoken in days, but I saw his brown eyes sparkle.

We all helped Harold's unparalyzed hand tear off the wrappings on the presents. Most of the time he kept reaching out and touching his red and white bike.

Harold lived one more month. By Christmas he was unconscious. The day after he died. The days that followed his death seemed twice as long as any other days I remember. My mind ached with thoughts of death, God and heaven. One Sunday when Harold's brother and sisters started out for Sunday school as usual, I walked down the street with them. When I reached the storefront meeting hall I could not turn away. I went in and stayed for church.

Sunday after Sunday, I went back, not only because I knew that Harold had been happy there, or because Harold's Sunday school teacher and others smiled and shook my hand. I went back to the church service because I knew I could find Jesus and peace of mind there.

The following Easter as I heard the invitation to accept Jesus Christ as my own personal Saviour, I edged past the woman sitting next to me and walked slowly down the aisle to kneel at the altar. "I want to be saved," I said humbly and was taken into a quiet, small room. "I want to come to God through Jesus Christ."

Now that I have accepted Christ as my Saviour, I know, as Harold must have known, that heaven is more than golden bicycles. My bitterness is gone and now that Christmas is here again I know its true meaning. In taking away my son at Christmas God opened the way to give me the greatest gift of all, eternal life. And I know Harold would have wanted it that way.

Harriet Balben

In Thine Own Heart

Though Christ a thousand times
In Bethlehem be born,
If He's not born in thee
Thy soul is still forlorn.
The cross on Golgotha
Will never save thy soul,
The cross in thine own heart
Alone can make thee whole.

Angelius Silesius

Heaven

"The Heavens Declare the Glory of God"

You ask me how I know it's true
  That there is a living God—
A God who rules the universe,
  The sky . . . the sea . . . the sod;
A God who holds all creatures
  In the hollow of His hand;
A God who put *Infinity*
  In one tiny grain of sand;
A God who made the seasons—
  Winter, Summer, Fall and Spring,
And put His flawless rhythm
  Into each created thing;
A God who hangs the sun out
  Slowly with the break of day,
And gently takes the stars in
  And puts the night away;
A God whose mighty handiwork
  Defies the skill of man,
For no achitect can alter
  God's *Perfect Master Plan*—
What better answers are there
  To prove His Holy Being
Than the wonders all around us
  That are ours just for the seeing.

Helen Steiner Rice

What Is Age

Age is opportunity no less
Than youth itself, though in another dress.
And as the evening twilight fades away,
The sky is filled with stars invisible by day.

Henry Wadsworth Longfellow

Mother's Last Letter

Mother had died on Christmas Day and I was just back at my home in Southern California following the funeral.

I leafed through the stack of mail which awaited me. There were cards of sympathy, thoughtful little notes from friends—but suddenly I found in the midst of them a card which was different. It was a birthday card.

Holding it in my hand, it suddenly came back to me. It had been on my birthday that the call had come—the word that my mother had suffered a sudden stroke.

I opened the card, looked at the familiar handwriting . . . and at once realized what this was. This was a card from my mother—a card which apparently had been in the mails on its way to me at the very moment that I was rushing to her side.

You can imagine how eagerly I read the little personal note she had penned on the back . . . for I realized that this was the last thing she had ever said to me.

Yes, my mother had never regained consciousness during those days until she awoke in Heaven in the presence of the One Whom she had loved so much and served so faithfully . . . and so these were her last words to me.

As I read them, the last phrase especially caught and gripped my attention. Writing on the first day of what proved to be her last week of conscious life, she commented on the busyness of the season and then ended with these words: "I must make the time count this week."

What a wonderful way, I thought, to begin one's last week of life: "I must make the time count."

Mother's fatal illness was sudden, unexpected. I really don't believe she had any particular apprehension of what was ahead as she wrote those words. I don't think she had any particular reason to write to me except for her usual cheerful busyness in "redeeming the time."

But I carry those words with me everywhere I go. I carry that little card in my Bible, and this reminder goes with me throughout the world.

And over and over again, as I think of those words, I thank God for one priceless gift He gives us.

Have you ever thought about it? Each day of our lives we receive a gift—a priceless gift—which comes from a royal source. It comes to us bright and sparkling, absolutely untouched, unspoiled.

What is this gift? The priceless gift of time.

Yes, time. Each day we receive a fresh, new supply—24 hours—1,440 minutes—86,400 seconds. Twenty-four hours we have never lived before; twenty-four hours we shall never live again.

What a wonderful attitude for one to have in facing his last week—or his last day or month or year: "I must make the time count."

Larry Ward

God's Work

What we see here of this world is but an expression of God's will, so to speak—a beautiful earth and sky and sea—beautiful affections and sorrows, wonderful changes and developments of creation, suns rising, stars shining, birds singing, clouds and shadows changing and fading, people loving each other, smiling and crying, the multiplied phenomena of Nature, multiplied in fact and fancy, in Art and Science, in every way that a man's intellect or education or imagination can be brought to bear. —And who is to say that we are to ignore all this, or not value them and love them, because there is another unknown world yet to come? Why that unknown future world is but a manifestation of God Almighty's will, and a development of Nature, neither more or less than this in which we are, and an angel glorified or a sparrow on a gutter are equally parts of His creation. The light upon all the saints in Heaven is just as much and no more God's work, as the sun which shall shine tomorrow upon this infinitesimal speck of creation.

William Makepeace Thackeray

From a Loved One in Heaven

I would not have you grieve for me today In memory of Walter.
Nor weep beside my vacant chair,
Could you but know my daily portion here
You would not, could not, wish me there.

I know now why He said, "Ear hath not heard."
I have no words, no alphabet.
Or even if I had I dare not tell
Because you could not bear it yet.

So, only this—I am the same, though changed,
Like Him! A joy more rich and strong
Than I had dreamed that any heart could hold,
And all my life is one glad song.

Sometimes when you are talking to our Lord
He turns and speaks to me . . . Dear heart,
In that rare moment you and I are just
The distance of a word apart!

And so my loved ones, do not grieve for me
Around the family board today;
Instead, rejoice, for we are one in Him,
And so I am not far away.

Martha Snell Nicholson

Played a Hymn on the Deck of a Sinking Boat

"Wallace H. Hartley
Died April 15, 1912
'Nearer, my God, to Thee'"

Such was the simple inscription on the rosewood coffin of one of the heroic figures of the musical realm, whose name was carried all over the world when the *Titanic* was sunk. As the boats were hurrying away from the wreck the marine band continued to play until their instruments were choked by the swirling water that closed about the musicians and sent them to heroes' graves. Of the eight bandsmen six were Englishmen, one a German and one a Frenchman.

Their leader was Mr. Wallace H. Hartley. One who had been with him on twenty-two voyages on the *Mauretania* states that he once casually asked him what he would do if he were on a boat which was wrecked. He promptly replied that he would play "Nearer, my God, to Thee." And this was the hymn he led the bandsmen in playing after they had long been rendering popular tunes, when he had to make a last selection before the great ship made her final plunge.

Among the 815 passengers and 688 crew who were drowned was W. T. Stead, editor of *The Review of Reviews.* A few years previous he had published *"Hymns That Have Helped."* In this list of the best hundred hymns, "Nearer, my God, to Thee" stands seventh. The Prince of Wales, later King Edward VII, sent a letter to the editor in which he expressed a preference for this hymn and said, "There is none more touching nor one that goes more truly to the heart than No. 7 on your list." Mr. Stead made the terse comment, "The hymn is as dear to the peasant as it is to the prince."

After the Battle of Fort Donelson, fought during the War between the States, a little drummer boy, whose arm had been shot away and whose life was ebbing away in a crimson tide, was found by his comrades. Even as he was dying he sang,

Still all my song shall be
Nearer, my God, to Thee,
Nearer to Thee.

The tune "Bethany" by Lowell Mason was written for this hymn; indeed, without it the hymn would not have been so widely accepted and sung.

President McKinley's last words were, "'Nearer, my God, to Thee,

E'en tho' it be a cross,' has been my constant prayer." The hymn was sung at his funeral. The sympathy for the long-suffering, wounded president broke forth on the day of his burial in the singing of this hymn on the streets, in street-cars, during the hours of his funeral:

Nearer, My God, to Thee

Nearer, my God, to Thee,
Nearer to Thee!
E'en though it be a cross
That raiseth me;
Still all my song shall be,
Nearer, my God, to Thee,
Nearer to Thee!

Though like the wanderer,
The sun gone down,
Darkness be over me,
My rest a stone;
Yet in my dreams I'd be
Nearer, my God, to Thee,
Nearer to Thee!

There let the way appear
Steps unto Heaven,
All that Thou send'st me
In mercy given;
Angels to beckon me
Nearer, my God, to Thee,
Nearer to Thee!

Then, with my waking thoughts
Bright with Thy praise,
Out of my stony griefs,
Bethel I'll raise;
So by my woes to be
Nearer, my God, to Thee,
Nearer to Thee!

Or if, on joyful wing,
Cleaving the sky,
Sun, moon and stars forgot,
Upward I fly,
Still all my song shall be,
Nearer, my God, to Thee,
Nearer to Thee!

Sarah Flower Adams

The Resurrection and The Life

Here on this earth we are gathered together in families. Our loved ones become inexpressibly precious to us. We live in intimate associations. One gets so close to mother and father, wife or husband, sons and daughters, that they literally become a part of one's life. Then comes a day when a strange change comes over one we love.

He is transformed before our very eyes. The light of life goes out of him. He cannot speak to us nor we to him. He is gone and we are left stunned and heartbroken. An emptiness and loneliness comes into our hearts. We broken-heartedly say, "That one whom I loved is dead." It is such a cold, hopeless thing to realize.

Then, out of the very depths of our despair, like the melody of music coming from a mighty organ, like the refreshing sound of rippling waters, comes that marvelous declaration of our Lord. "I am the resurrection, and the life: he that believeth in me, though he were dead, yet shall he live: and whosoever liveth and believeth in me shall never die."

Then we know! We *know* we have not lost our loved ones who have died in the Lord. We have been separated, and so long as we live there will be an empty place left in our hearts. To some extent, the loneliness will always be there. But when we really know that one is not forever lost, it does take away the sorrow. There is a vast difference between precious memories, loneliness, the pain of separation, on the one hand, and a sorrow that ruins and blights our lives, on the other hand.

Charles L. Allen

Not only in my summer let me sing
When Beauty storms my senses and my soul,
When mine is the mysterious and dark
Delight of one who feels the quivering
Tumultuous heart surrender utterly,
Idolatrous of that bright deity.
Let me not ever lose the moment when
I stand, transfigured, on the shining verge
Of dreams beyond all telling and I glimpse
The realm where earth and heaven subtly merge.
O God, when in my winter I shall walk
The quiet and the twilight ways along,
Let me feel still a breath upon my brow
And find in snow the silver seeds of song.

Adelaide Love

Heaven

Some time ago, Dr. Charles E. Fuller of the Old Fashioned Revival Hour announced that he would speak the next Sunday on "Heaven." When that time came, he read the following letter just received from Dr. Harry Rimmer, the noted scientist and Bible teacher, who had been hospitalized for throat cancer.

"Next Sunday, you are to talk about Heaven. I am interested in that land, because I have held a clear title to a bit of property there for more than 55 years. I did not buy it. It was given to me 'without money and without price.' But the donor purchased it for me at a tremendous sacrifice. I am not holding it for speculation, since the title is not transferable. It is not a vacant lot.

"For more than half a century I have been sending materials out of which the Great Architect and Builder of the Universe has been building a home for me, a home which will never be remodeled nor repaired, because it will suit me perfectly, individually, and will never grow old. Termites can never undermine its foundations, for they rest upon the Rock of Ages. Fire cannot destroy it. Floods cannot wash it away. No locks nor bolts will ever be placed on its doors, for no vicious person can ever enter that Land where my dwelling stands, now almost completed and almost ready for me to enter in and abide in peace eternally, without fear of being ejected.

"There is a valley of deep shadows between the place where I live in California and that to which I shall journey in a very short time. I cannot reach my home in that city of gold without passing through this dark valley of shadows; but I am not afraid, because the best friend I ever had went through the same valley long, long ago and drove away all its gloom. He has stuck by me through thick and thin since we first became acquainted 55 years ago, and I hold His promise in printed form that He will never forsake me nor leave me alone. He will be with me as I walk through the valley of shadows, and I shall not lose my way when He is with me.

"I hope to hear your sermon on Heaven next Sunday from my home in Los Angeles, but I have no assurance that I shall be able to do so. My ticket to Heaven has no date marked for the journey, no return coupon, and no permit for baggage. Yes, I am all ready to go, and I may not be here while you are talking next Sunday—but I shall meet you Over There some day."

Dr. Rimmer, though a brilliant scientist, had a beautifully simple faith in Christ as his Saviour. He believed what Jesus Christ said: "I go to prepare a place for you. And if I go and prepare a place for you, I will come again, and receive you unto myself: that where I am, there ye may be also . . . I am the way, the truth, and the life; no man cometh unto the Father, but by me."

It was not long before he was ushered into the presence of his beloved Lord whom he so greatly loved and devotedly served and where his letter became reality and faith became sight.

The Eternal Goodness

I dimly guess from blessings known
  Of greater out of sight,
And, with the chastened Psalmist, own
  His judgments too are right.

I know not what the future hath
  Of marvel or surprise,
Assured alone that life and death
  His mercy underlies.

And if my heart and flesh are weak
  To bear an untried pain,
The bruised reed he will not break,
  But strengthen and sustain.

No offering of my own I have,
  Nor works my faith to prove;
I can but give the gifts he gave,
  And plead his love for love.

And so beside the Silent Sea
  I wait the muffled oar;
No harm from him can come to me
  On ocean or on shore.

I know not where his islands lift
  Their fronded palms in air;
I only know I cannot drift
  Beyond his love and care.

And Thou, O Lord! by whom are seen
  Thy creatures as they be,
Forgive me if too close I lean
  My human heart on Thee!

John Greenleaf Whittier

The Threshold Years

Now that I am seventy years old, and life is rapidly passing for me, if I should be asked how my discovery of the unselfishness of God affects my feelings towards old age and death, I could but say, that, secure in the knowledge that God is and that He is enough, I find old age delightful in the present, and death a prospect for the future.

If it were not for Him, old age with its failing powers and its many infirmities could not but be a sad and wearisome time; but, with God, our lovely unselfish God, at the back of it, old age is simply a delightful resting-place.

I have tried in my day to help bear the burdens of my own generation, and, now that that generation has almost passed away, I am more than happy to know that the responsibilities of the present generation do not rest upon me.

I admire the divine order that evidently lays upon each generation its own work, to be done in its own way; and I am convinced that, whether it may seem to us for good or for ill, the generation that is passing must give place to the one that is coming and must keep hands off from interfering.

Everything is safe when an unselfish love is guiding and controlling, and therefore my old heart is at rest, and I can lay down my arms with a happy confidence that, since God is in His heaven, all must necessarily be right with His world. And I can peacefully wait to understand what seems mysterious now, until the glorious day of revelation to which every hour brings me nearer.

Therefore with an easy mind I can look forward to death, and the prospect of leaving this life and of entering into the larger and grander life beyond is pure bliss to me. It is like having a new country, full of unknown marvels, to explore; and the knowledge that no one and nothing can hinder my going there is a secret spring of joy at the bottom of my heart.

I am like the butterfly just preparing to slip out of its old cocoon; panting for the life outside, but with no experience to tell it what kind of life that outside life will be. But I believe with all my heart that the apostle told the truth when he declared that, "Eye hath not seen, nor ear heard, neither hath it entered into the heart of man the things which God hath prepared for them that love him" (I Cor. 2:9). And what better prospect could the soul have!

Then will be fulfilled the prayer of our Lord, "Father, I will that they also, whom thou hast given me, be with me where I am; that they may behold my glory which thou hast given me" (John 17:24).

That glory is not the glory of dazzling light but it is the glory of unselfish love. I have had a few faint glimpses of this glory now and here, and it has been enough to ravish my heart. But there I shall see Him as He is, in all the glory of an infinite unselfishness which no heart of man has even been able to conceive; and I await the moment with joy.

Hannah Whitall Smith

Joy and Peace in Believing

Sometimes a light surprises
  The Christian while he sings;
It is the Lord who rises
  With healing in his wings:
When comforts are declining,
  He grants the soul again
A season of clear shining
  To cheer it after rain.

In holy contemplation,
  We sweetly then pursue
The theme of God's salvation,
  And find it ever new:
Set free from present sorrow,
  We cheerfully can say,
E'en let th' unknown tomorrow
  Bring with it what it may.

It can bring with it nothing
  But he will bear us thro';
Who gives the lilies clothing
  Will clothe his people too:
Beneath the spreading heavens,
  No creature but is fed;
And he who feeds the ravens
  Will give his children bread.

Though vine, nor fig tree neither,
  Their wonted fruit should bear,
Tho' all the fields should wither,
  Nor flocks, nor herds, be there:
Yet God the same abiding,
  His praise shall tune my voice;
For while in him confiding,
  I cannot but rejoice.

William Cowper

The Heavens Declare Thy Glory, Lord!

[*Psalm XIX*]

The heavens declare thy glory, Lord!
  In every star thy wisdom shines;
But when our eyes behold thy word,
  We read thy name in fairer lines.

The rolling sun, the changing light,
  And nights and days thy power confess;
But the blest volume thou has writ
  Reveals thy justice and thy grace.

Isaac Watts

Dying Words of Saints

Gordon Hall, far from home, dying in the door of a heathen temple, said: "Glory to thee, O God!"

What did dying Wilberforce say to his wife? *"Come and sit beside me, and let us talk of Heaven. I never knew what happiness was until I found Christ."*

What did dying Hannah More say? *"To go to Heaven—think what that is! To go to Christ, who died that I might live! Oh, glorious grave! Oh, what a glorious thing it is to die! Oh, the love of Christ!"*

What did Mr. Toplady, the great hymn-writer, say in his last hour? "Who can measure the depths of the third heaven? Oh, the sunshine that fills my soul! I shall soon be gone, for surely no one can live in this world after such glories as God has manifested to my soul."

Sir Charles Hare, in his last moment had such a rapturous vision that he cried: "Upward! upward! upward!"

But grander than that was the testimony of St. Paul, when, in the Mamartine dungeon, he cried: "I am now ready to be offered, and the time of my departure is at hand; I have fought a good fight, I have finished my course, I have kept the faith; henceforth there is laid up for me a crown of righteousness, which the Lord, the righteous judge, will give me in that day, and not to me only, but to all them that love his appearing!"

The noted Dr. T. DeWitt Talmadge said, "We are speeding toward the last hour of our earthly residence. When I see the sunset I say: 'One day less to live.' When I close this Bible, Sunday night, I say: 'Another Lord's day departed.' When I bury a friend, I say: 'Another earthly attraction gone forever.'

"What nimble feet the years have! From decade to decade, they go at a bound. There is a place for us, whether marked or not, where you and I will sleep the last sleep, and the men are now living who will with solemn tread, carry us to our resting-place. Aye, it is known in Heaven whether our departure will be a coronation or a banishment.

"Once when I was in danger of going down at sea my own life suddenly seemed utterly unsatisfactory. I could only say, 'Here, Lord, take me as I am. I cannot mend matters now. Lord Jesus, thou didst die for the chief of sinners. That's me! It seems, Lord, as though my work is done, and poorly done, and upon thy infinite mercy I cast myself, and in this hour of shipwreck and darkness commit myself and her whom I hold by the hand to thee, O Lord Jesus! praying that it may be a short struggle in the water, and that at the same instant we may both arrive in glory!' Oh! I tell you a man prays straight to the mark when he has a cyclone above him, an ocean beneath him, and eternity close to him.

"And may God grant that, when all our days on earth are ended, we may find that, in the rich mercy of our Lord Jesus Christ, we all have weathered the gale!"

GOLDEN NUGGETS

Do you know that your bodies are made of some of the same substances that are found in the sun and the other stars? You are a sample of the great Universe. So do not let little things trouble you but think and act as if you were a part of a bigger world than the little earth upon which you live.

Edwin B. Frost

Eternal life is much more than eternal existence. It implies happiness, vigor, peace, and all that makes life worth living. It is the divine life which is implanted in us when we are born of the Spirit and become children of God. It begins in this life, but, being divine and natural, it endures forever. It is life that belongs to heaven, which inspires all heavenly beings and makes heaven what it is.

Francis N. Peloubet

Understanding

I did not know, till 'neath the rod
I passed, how sore I needed God;
In sorrow's night, lo! like a star
I saw His love shine from afar.

I did not know, until above
God called the idol of my love
Beyond the reach of yearning eyes,
How beautiful is Paradise.

Charles Kingsley

golden lives

A Teenage Triumph

KAREN RUTH JOHNSON
March 31, 1942 - June 6, 1959

"For to me to live is Christ, and to die is gain."
PHIL. 1:21

This paper was prepared by Karen Ruth Johnson, fulfilling a school assignment at San Marino High School in Southern California. It is of special interest that it was completed on Thursday night, June 4, and presented to her teacher on Friday, June 5. On Saturday, June 6th, Karen's earthly life ceased as the result of a head-on automobile collision. Karen's high school diploma was awarded posthumously at the graduation exercises of her class on Wednesday, June 17, 1959. Karen found the Christian life exciting. She walked with God joyously and exuberantly. Her brief life is a triumphant testimony to the reality of life in Christ.

June 5, 1959

MY PHILOSOPHY OF LIFE
by Karen Ruth Johnson

My philosophy of life is based on the Holy Bible and the God that wrote it. I know that He has a plan for my life and through daily prayer and reading of His Word I will be able to see it. As far as my life work or life partner I am leaving it in His hands and am willing to do anything He says.

I feel that this philosophy is very practical and can be applied to everyday life. Every decision can be taken to the Lord in prayer and the peace that comes from knowing Jesus Christ as my personal Saviour is something many cannot understand. Many search for a purpose and reason for life. I know that I am on this earth to have fellowship with God and to win others to the saving knowledge of His Son, Jesus Christ. I know that after death I will go to be with Him forever.

Jesus Christ teaches love and respect for everyone throughout the New Testament and we are not to judge anyone because He will on the judgment day. In God's sight no one person is worth any more than another.

Knowing and loving Jesus Christ personally makes me want to please Him and accomplish things for His glory. Paul says in the New Testament, "Whatsoever ye do, do it all to the glory of God" and "For me, to live is Christ, to die is gain."

This philosophy contains all the seven points given in your lecture of April 20th. As I stated in the beginning, it is very:

(1) practical to have someone to turn to for any decision or problem, small or large. What could be more

(2) optimistic than knowing that God has a purpose and a plan for one's life and is willing to keep in constant fellowship with anyone who will. To know I have accepted Jesus Christ's gift of Salvation and will have eternal life in Heaven is a most wonderful thing and brings peace to my heart. God has the best for us and if we let Him He will improve our lives and solve our problems.

(3) God in His Holy Word teaches us to have love and burden for every person as Jesus Christ Himself.

(4) One of my main purposes in life is to share this experience I have had with Christ and to show them the peace and happiness that it brings.

(5) This is an important goal in itself, but more completely, my aim in life is to accomplish what the Lord has for me to do, which is certainly the most worthwhile goal in life.

(6) The closer I grow to Him the more happiness I find and the busier I am. He has things for me that the world could never offer and I learn to appreciate more and more how fortunate I am.

(7) God's standards are higher than anything attainable and present a great challenge and make me realize how futile it would be for me to do the best I could, because I, being human, could never reach God's standards, and therefore never be worthy of entering Heaven. God has given me contact with the best; in His world, in my born again friends, and in my fellowship with Jesus Christ. It is well known that the highest beauty, truth, justice, and goodness is found in God's Word.

This is my philosophy, and yet it is not mine, but I am God's, and whatever I have is His and I have faith that He is the only answer and I do love Him so.

Contributed by Karen's family in the hope that it will have real meaning to teenagers and others who seek to make an honest appraisal of life.

I Never Saw a Moor

I never saw a moor,
I never saw the sea;
Yet know I how the heather looks,
And what a wave must be.
I never spoke with God,
Nor visited in heaven;
Yet certain am I of the spot
As if the chart were given.

Emily Dickinson

Crossing the Bar

Sunset and evening star,
  And one clear call for me!
And may there be no moaning of the bar,
  When I put out to sea,

But such a tide as moving seems asleep,
  Too full for sound and foam,
When that which drew from out the boundless deep
  Turns again home.

Twilight and evening bell,
  And after that the dark!
And may there be no sadness of farewell,
  When I embark;

For tho' from out our bourne of Time and Place
  The flood may bear me far,
I hope to see my Pilot face to face
  When I have crost the bar.

Alfred Tennyson

Heaven

Life changes all our thoughts of heaven;
At first we think of streets of gold,
  Of gates of pearl and dazzling light,
Of shining wings and robes of white,
  And things all strange to mortal sight.

But in the afterward of years
  It is a more familiar place,
A home unhurt by sighs or tears,
  Where waiteth many a well-known face.

With passing months it comes more near,
  It grows more real day by day,
Not strange or cold, but very dear—
  The glad homeland not far away.

Robert Browning

Dear Friend,

Have you ever thought of all the changes going on in the world these days? It seems that all around us we see new and different things. There are new countries coming into existence, new products on the market, new foods, new medicines—even new math!

One aspect of change in our country today is the fact that people are frequently on the move from one place to another. Perhaps you or other members of your family have found it necessary to move on several occasions. Recently I read of one man who had changed his residence nine times in eleven years! And some people move even more often that that.

The Scriptures tell us that although change and movement are a part of life in this world, there are some things that are unchanging and eternal. We know, for example, that God's Word is eternally fixed and lasts forever. We also know that the love of God for His people is constant and unchanging. Through the prophet Jeremiah, God says . . ."I have loved thee with an *everlasting* love." (Jer. 31:3).

One of the thrilling features of this love is that God has prepared a glorious, *permanent* home for those who trust and obey him. This beautiful home is called Heaven. It is a land of life everlasting and of happiness beyond anything we can now understand.

But God has planned Heaven as a place of joy for those who are *prepared* to go there. Are *you* prepared for that wonderful place?

Preparing for Heaven does not mean what a lot of people think. It has nothing to do with doing enough "good" to offset the "bad" we have done. It goes beyond denominational lines; goes beyond confirmation, baptism, or church membership; it is not bound by race, color or creed.

Personally, I know I'll be in that land some day; not because of any good thing that I've done—but because Jesus Christ has paid for my salvation, and offered it to me as a free gift, which I accepted.

I hope you'll be there too. God wants you to be there, and you can be there by coming to Him through His Son, Jesus Christ—as I did seventeen wonderful years ago. The way is made so clear by Jesus Who said, "I am the Way, the Truth, and the Life; no man cometh unto the Father but by Me." (St. John 14:6).

May the Holy Spirit impress upon you the importance, the urgency, the necessity of your settling once and for all the great question, "Will I go to Heaven when I die?"

We have all been wrong in many things, but we cannot afford to be wrong in this; the price is too high, the cost too great.

If you are not sure of the answer to this question and would like to be, just write and tell me, and I'll send you free, a wonderful and comforting 32 page booklet entitled "Heaven." I'm sure this will be a real blessing in helping you on the way to the Father's home above.

Most sincerely,

Arthur DeMoss

Arthur DeMoss